HURLEY
NEW YORK

HURLEY
NEW YORK
A BRIEF HISTORY

Deana F. Decker

The History Press

Published by The History Press
Charleston, SC 29403
www.historypress.net

First published 2009

Manufactured in the United States

ISBN 978.1.59629.699.2

Library of Congress Cataloging-in-Publication Data

Decker, Deana F.
Hurley, New York : a brief history / Deana F. Decker.
p. cm.
Includes bibliographical references.
ISBN 978-1-59629-699-2
1. Hurley (N.Y. : Town)--History. 2. Hurley (N.Y. : Town)--Social life and customs. I. Title.
F129.H95D44 2009
974.7'34--dc22
2009039730

To my husband, Vince; my kids, Megan and Thomas; my family; and the girls of the Cosmopolitan Coffee Club, Jessica, Corina, Nicole, Sue and Sarah. I love you all for all of your support and friendship.

CONTENTS

PREFACE

While creating my first book, *Images of America Hurley*, I found a lack of publications focusing solely on Hurley. Most of the time, it is included as an afterthought to Kingston, the Catskill Mountains or even the Hudson Valley. Many times, it is not included at all. Therefore, I felt the need to create a more detailed history of our beautiful, diverse town.

A few things to note about this book: Most of the information about the people and houses comes from my files in the town historian's office, thanks to the hard work of my predecessors, Olive Clearwater, John Hofler and David Baker. This information is by no means complete. This book is only a quick look at the broad picture of this history-filled area.

The spelling of the settlers' names is an art unto itself. Even the simplest of names has multiple variations. People had different levels of education, ranging from the well educated to the illiterate. Spellings varied from literal to phonetic. A mix of cultures added to these variations. I have attempted to keep one spelling for ease of reading, unless I am quoting an early author.

A note about Dutch names: The Dutch did not use surnames. Their last names were derived from their fathers' first names. For example, Thomas, son of Jan, would have the name Thomas Jansen. His son, Cornelis, would take the name Cornelis Thomassen, and so on. An *s* or *se* is added. They would also add, as a last name, the land where they came from in Holland.

INTRODUCTION

In 1609, during the heyday of world exploration, the Dutch East India Company sent English explorer Henry Hudson to find a northeast passage to Asia. Unsuccessful, Hudson and his crew crossed the Atlantic Ocean on the ship the *Half Moon* to find a northwest passage. They found a wide, long river that now bears Hudson's name. He sailed as far as present-day Albany and claimed all of the land between it and Manhattan Island. Hudson encountered the local natives. Relations between the Europeans and the natives were amicable, and they traded many goods, including furs.

In 1614, the newly formed New Netherland Company received a grant from the Dutch government for the territory between New France and Virginia. Interested in the fur trade, the Dutch West India Company, chartered in 1621, established a trading post at Beverwyck (Albany), north of Fort Orange, and New Amsterdam (New York City) ten years later.

Dutch settlement proved slow since life in the Netherlands was very comfortable. It was difficult to convince Dutch burghers (citizens) to leave their homes to travel across a wide ocean and work as tenant farmers on land owned by an aristocrat. These patroons offered little hope of improving one's life. Why start over in the wilderness when life in your homeland provided religious tolerance and a bountiful agricultural system?

In some sources I consulted, two years of reference for settlement are given. There was a change in the calendar affecting the days between December 31 and March 25 for the years prior to 1753. In many cases, a reference to a year may not have been updated.

The following is a list of some of the earliest settlers who had an impact on Hurley. Other settlers and their families are listed later in the book, as the time they arrived in the area corresponds with the book's timeline.

MATTHEW BLANCHAN (about 1610–1687) was born at Noueville-au-Corne, Artois, France. He moved to Armentieres on the Belgian border, where he married Magdeleine Jorisse in 1633. They, along with their daughters, Catherine (1635–1696) and Marie (1640–1679), moved to Canterbury, England. There, in 1647, their daughter Magdalena was born. Elizabeth was born in 1651, and Matthew Jr. followed in 1655. Magdalena married Jan Matthys Jansen of Fort Orange in 1667, and they had ten children. Elizabeth married Pieter Cornelisz Louw, and they had nine children. She then married Jan Foockens Heermance. Matthew married Margrietje Christina Vas VanSchoonhoven, and they had eight children.

After the trial and execution of Charles I in 1649, Charles Louis regained power. He found many cities in ruin. He offered many inducements to Huguenot merchants and manufacturers in northern France to move to Germany. By 1651, Blanchan was among a large group of French Huguenots who moved to Mannheim, Germany. In 1655, Catherine married Louis du Bois. Marie married Antoine Crispell in 1660. Later that year, the family, except for Catherine and Louis, boarded *De Vergulde Otter* (the *Gilded Otter*) and headed for the New Netherlands. The passenger list reads, "Mattheus Blanchand, farmer, from Artois, wife and three children, 12, 9, and 3 years old. Anthony Krypel, farmer, from Artois, and wife."[1]

The travelers were welcomed by Peter Stuyvesant, who gave them a letter directing that they be provided with food and shelter upon their arrival at the Esopus. Louis and Catherine joined their family in the New World in 1661. By April 1663, Matthew, Louis and Anthony had obtained land at Nieuw Dorp. Matthew accrued several more parcels of land in Wiltwyck and Nieuw Dorp over the next few years.

LAMBERT HUYBERTSE [BRINK] (1623–1702) was born in Holland. He left Wageningen and immigrated to New Amsterdam on December 23, 1659, on the ship *Geloove* (*Faith*) with his wife, Hendrikje Cornelisse, their son, Huybertse, and their daughter, Jannetje. Another son, Cornelis, was born during the voyage. To designate their homeland, Lambert's children used the last name Brink. After arriving in New Amsterdam, the family headed north to Esopus. In 1662, Lambert leased land in Nieuw Dorp. In 1667, when the lease was up, Lambert and his sons purchased this and other land in Hurley. Lambert served as a soldier in Captain Henry Pawling's army. He was a sheriff of Esopus. He was also an overseer for Stuyvesant's land at Esopus and at one time leased one of Stuyvesant's farms. In 1670, Lambert built the original part of the stone house that stands today on Wynkoop Road just west of the Esopus Creek.

Children:
Huybert (1655–?) married Hendrickje Swartwout of Albany in 1686, and they had eight children.
Jannetje (1657–?) married Corn Tannise Cool in 1658 and had one child.
Cornelis (1660–?) married Marritje Egberts Meyndentsen of New York in 1685 and had eleven children.
Hendrick Lambertsen (1663–?) married Gersje Jansen and had one child.
Lysbeth Lamberts (1666–?) married Arien Garretsen NewKirk in 1686. They had six children.
Gerrit Lambertsen (1668–?) married Antje Hooghlandt, and their children assumed the surname Teerpening.
Pieter Lambertsen (1670–?) married Geertny Tennisen Matthewssen (van Newkirk) in 1692, and they had ten children.

ANTOINE CRISPELL (1635–1707) was born in St. Guin, Artois, France. He married Maria Blanchan (1640–1679), daughter of Matthew Blanchan, in Mannheim, Germany in 1660. They sailed on the *Gilded Otter* with her family in 1660 and arrived in Wildwyck in December. At first, Antoine worked as a farmhand, and in May 1661, he obtained a lot in Wildwyck.

Children:
Maria Magdelene (1662–after 1706) married Mattys Cornelis Slecht, son of Cornelis Barentsen Slecht, about 1681. They had nine children.
Pieter (1664–1696) married Neeltje Gerritsen Newkirk (1667–1706), daughter of Gerrit Cornelissen van Newkirk, in 1689. They had three children. After Pieter died, she married Johannes Schepmoes in 1697.
Lysbeth (1668–after 1709) married Elias Ean before 1697. They had five children.
Sara (1671–after 1710) married Huybert Suylandt of Hurley before 1696. They had five children.
Jan (1674–?) married Gerrtje Jans Roosa, daughter of Jan Roosa and Hillegonde Willhamus van Buren, in 1701. They had nine children.

Antoine then married Petronella Du Mond (1656–1707) in 1680. They had two children who died young.

Jannetie (1686–after 1727) married Nicholas Hoffman in 1704. They had nine children. Nicholas built the stone house on the corner of North Front and Green Streets in Kingston.

ANTHONY D'HOOGES (1622–1655) sailed to New Netherlands on *den Corinck David* in July 1641. He stayed in New Amsterdam and then journeyed north to Rensselaerswyck in 1642. From then until 1648, he worked as a business manager for the colony. He served as the secretary of the colony until his death. He married Eva Albertse Bratt in October 1647, and they had five children. In August 1657, Eva married Roelof Swartwout.

Children:

Maria (1648–?) first married Hendrick Bries, a shoemaker, and they had one child. She then married Jacob Lookerman, widower of Tryntje Classen, in 1696.

Anna (1650–?) married Warner Hornbeck. They had seven children, all born in Hurley.

Catrjna (1651–?) married Harmanus Rutgers, and they had three children.

Captain Johannes (1653–?) married Margarita Post in 1675. They had seven children, all born in Hurley. He was appointed captain in Hurley in 1689.

Eleanora (1655–?) first married Willem Mousnuer de la Montagne in 1673, and they had six children. She then married Cornelis de Duyster, and they had one child.

TJERCK CLAESEN DE WITT (?–1700) emigrated from northern Germany sometime in the 1650s. He married Barbara Andriessen van Amsterdam (1630?–1714) in 1656 in New Amsterdam. He is found in Albany court records in 1656 and 1657. In September 1660, Tjerck traded his Albany property for land in Wiltwyck. In 1669, Tjerck obtained land between Kingston and Hurley, where he built a house and barn. The house still stands today.

Children:

Captain Andries (1657–1710) married Jannetje Egbertsen, daughter of Egbert Meindertse and Jeepe Jans, in 1682. They had twelve children, including Johannes (1701–1776), who will be mentioned later. The captain died when two broken beams fell and crushed him.

Tjaatje (1659–before 1724) married Matthys Matthysen Van Keuren, son of Matthys Jansen Van Keuren and Margarete Hendtickse, in 1677. After the death of his father, his mother married Thomas Chambers.

Jannetje (1682–1744) married Cornelis Swits and had no children.

Klaes (1664–before 1698).

Jan (1666–before 1715) married Wyntje Kiersted, daughter of Roeloff Kierdted and Eyke Roosa. Eyke was the daughter of Aldert Heymans Roosa.

Geertruy (1668–?) married Hendrick Hendricksen Schoonmaker (1665–before 1718), son of Hendrick Jochemsen Schoonmaker and Elsie Janse, in 1688.

Jacob (?–after 1753) married Greetje Vernooy, daughter of Cornelius C. Vernooy and Annetje Cornelis. In 1705, he became a trustee of the town of Rochester in southern Ulster County.

Rachel (?–after 1738) married Cornelius Bogardus, son of Cornelius Bogardus Sr. and Helena Teller.

Lucas (?–1703) married Annetje Delva, daughter of Anthony Delve and Jannetje Hillebrants, in 1695. Widowed twice, she also married Gerrit van Benschoten in 1706 and then Hendrick Rosekrans in 1721.

Peerck (dates unknown) first married Maritje Jane Vandenbergin in 1698. He then married Maria Teunis, widow of Jacob Du Mott, in 1723.

Tereck (dates unknown) is only recorded in his father's will.

Maritje (dates unknown) first married Hendrick Hendricksen Kortreght, son of Hendrick Jansen and Catherine Hansen Webber, in 1700. She divorced him and married James Macklin in 1702.

Aagge (1684–?) married Jan Pawling, son of Henry Pauling and Neeltje Roosa, daughter of Aldert Heymans Roosa, in 1712.

LOUIS DU BOIS (1626–1696) was born near L'Ile, France. He married Catherine Blanchan, daughter of Matthew Blanchan, in 1655. They both died in Kingston. Catherine and Louis did not emigrate with her family but sailed on the *St. Jean Baptiste* and joined them in Esopus in 1661. Louis received a land grant in Nieuw Dorp in April 1663. They had twelve children, four of whom died young.

Children:

Abraham (1657–1731) married Margaret Deyo, daughter of Christian Deyo and Jeantje Verbeau, in 1681. They had eight children. Abraham served in the Second Canadian Expedition in Colonel Thomas Farmer's regiment.

Isaac (1659–1660) married Maria Hasbrouck (1644–1718), daughter of Jean Hasbrouck and Anna Deyo, in 1683.

Jacob (1661–1745) first married Lysbeth Vernooy, daughter of Cornelis Cornelissen Vernoy and Annatje Cornelis Van Der Cuyl, in 1689. They had one daughter, and Lysbeth died soon after giving birth. Jacob then married Gerritje Gerritsen van Newkirk, daughter of Gerrit Cornelisen Newkirk and Chieltje Gerritse, in 1691. They had ten children. Jacob lived in Hurley his whole life. He is listed in 1715 as a member of the Hurley Militia and as a town trustee in 1719.

Sarah (1662–1726) married Joost Jans Van Meteren (1656–1706), son of Jan Joosten Van Meteren and Maetken Hendricksen, in 1682. They had nine children. In many early records, his father is listed as Jans Joosten, who held many positions in Hurley and Marbletown. In 1673, he was elected one of the four magistrates of Hurley and Marbletown, and he served as justice of the peace.

David (1667–?) married Cornelia Vernooy, daughter of Cornelis Cornelissen Vernoy and Annatje Cornelis Van Der Cuyl, in 1689. They had six children. In 1715, David is listed as a member of Captain Vernooy's militia unit of Rochester and Wawarsing.

Solomon (1669–1759) married Tryntje Gerritse Foochen (1669–?), daughter of Gerrit Cornelissen and Jacomyntje Cornelissen Slecht, in 1692. They had nine children. Solomon served as a lieutenant in the militia and was a trustee of Kingston.

Louis Jr. (1677–1749) married Rachel Hasbrouck(1680–?), daughter of Abraham Hasbrouck and Maria Deyo, in 1701. They had seven children.

Mattheus (1679–1748) married Sara Matthysen Van Keuren (1678–?), daughter of Matthys Matthyssen Van Leuren and Taatje De Witt, in 1697. They had twelve children.

Magdelina (1680–?)

After the death of Louis, Catherine then married Jean Cottinm, former schoolmaster of New Paltz and Kingston merchant.

EVERT PELS emigrated from Stetten, Pomerania, and sailed for the New World in 1642. In 1647, he leased a farm on Papacanee Island for a six-year term. After building a new house and barn, he transferred the lease. He leased another farm until 1661, when he moved to Esopus and leased the saw- and gristmill in Greenbush, outside of Albany, formerly occupied by Jacob Jansz Flodder. Evert was one of the first *scheppen* (commissioners) of Wiltwyck. He married Jannetje Symens. He kept a store at Wiltwyck for a few years and eventually returned to Albany.

Children:

Sara married Jacob Aertsen Van Wagenen(1652–?), son of Aerent Jacobsen, in 1677.

Claartje (1651–?) married Gerrit Aertsen Van Wagenen (1651–1721), a brother and possibly twin to Jacob Aertsen, in 1670. He was a trustee of the Corporation of Kingston and owned twenty-six acres in Wiltwyck.

ALDERT HEYMANS ROOSA (1610–?) was born in Herwinan, Guilderland, Holland. Aldert, with his wife, Wyntje Ariens (1622–1710), and eight children, boarded the ship *De Bonte Koe* (the *Spotted Cow*) in Holland in 1660 and sailed to the New Netherlands. Within a month, the family headed up the Hudson River and settled in Wiltwyck. Being a wealthy man, Aldert quickly attained influence in Wiltwyck. Peter Stuyvesant appointed him as commissioner and magistrate. In 1662, Aldert was in charge of overseeing the establishment of Nieuw Dorp and subsequently moved there with his family.

Children:

Hyman Akdertse (1643–1708) first married an unknown wife before 1675. In 1678, he married Anna Margariet Claasen Roosevelt (1654–1706), daughter of Nicholas Roosevelt. They had eight children.

Arie Alderts (1645–1715) first married Weyntie Aendriaanz d'Joog, who died between 1682 and 1684. He then married Martje Pels, daughter of Evert Pels, in 1684. They had ten children.

Jan Aldertse (1646–1736) married Hillegonde Willensen van Buren (1653–1725) in 1671. They had fourteen children. Jan was a blacksmith, and by 1670, at the age of twenty-four, he had purchased his own land, built a one-room cottage in Nieuw Dorp and possibly had a shop on the property. Jan followed his father's example of public service; he was listed in 1708 as a Hurley town official, and he joined the Hurley Militia.

Eyke (1651–1684) married Roeloff Kiersted (1647–1710) in 1670. They had nine children.

Maritje (1652–?) married Laurens Jansen von Kortryck Low (1651–1727) in 1672. They had nine children.

Neetje (1653–after October 1745) married Captain Henry Pauling in 1676. They had eight children.

Jannitje (1656–1726) married Mattys Ten Eyck (1658–1754) in 1679. They had eight children.

Chapter One

SETTLING THE 'SOPUS

The first known land deed for the area known as Esopus was written on June 5, 1652, at Fort Orange between Captain Thomas Chambers and Esopus natives Kawachhikan and Sowappekat, who represented their tribe. The grant states, in part, that the natives

> *do grant and convey to Thomas Chambers, residing about the fortress of Fort Orange certain parcel of land situated in the Esopus above named extending Southwest and Northeast named Machetapacick, Nethainekoeck, Sepeeckcoe, Narenmapth, Wiwisowachkick, with a path from the said land to the river, and the grantors claim declared to have been satisfied and paid from the same.*

Shortly thereafter, many more such transactions transpired between the Esopus natives and the Europeans. They traded their lands for many different items, including metal knives, hatchets and alcohol. This exposure of the natives to alcohol played an integral role in future conflicts between the two groups.

There is evidence that people have inhabited the Hudson Valley for thousands of years. The Lenapes—the Europeans called them the Delawares—lived in small villages and farmed the fertile flood plains of the Esopus, Rondout and Wallkill Creeks before Chambers and others moved into the area. These Indians are locally referred to as the Esopus Indians.

At first, relations between these diverse cultures were friendly, and they traded many goods. The Lenapes did not understand the European concept of buying and selling the land, which they depended on for their survival. Increased colonization, disrespectful treatment and greater access to and weakness for alcohol began to create conflict between the groups.

The growing tensions pushed Stuyvesant to order the settlers to build a stockade and to construct their homes inside it. The settlers disregarded this order and continued living on their spread-out farms. An incident on May 1, 1658, conveyed in a letter written by Thomas Chambers, recounts the events that led to the settlers' decision to build the stockade:

> *I saw that the savages had an anker* [ten-gallon keg] *of brandy lying under a tree. I tasted myself and found it pure brandy. About dusk, they fired at and killed Harmen Jacobsen who was standing in a yacht in the river; and during the night, they set fire to the house of Jacob Adrijansa, and the people were compelled to flee for their lives. Once before we were driven away and expelled from our property, as long as we are under the jurisdiction of the West India Company we ask your assistance as Esopus could feed the whole of New Netherland. I have informed myself among the Indians who killed Harmen, and they have promised to deliver the savage in bonds. Please do not begin the war too suddenly, and not until we have constructed a stronghold for defense.*[2]

On May 3, an agreement was reached to build a stockade, combine the scattered homes and build inside the protected area. In June, under the supervision of Stuyvesant, the settlers built the stockade in the area now known as the Stockade District of Kingston. After its completion, Stuyvesant left, but he stationed there a garrison of twenty-four soldiers commanded by Sergeant Andries Lourensen. This garrison had grown to fifty soldiers by the end of the year, when tensions with the Indians once again increased. In September 1659, Stuyvesant dispatched Ensign Dirck Smit to Esopus with additional soldiers and arms. Smit became the new commander and remained so until his death in 1660.[3]

THE FIRST ESOPUS WAR

Inevitably, tensions finally hit their peak in 1659. On September 20, Thomas Chambers paid wages to four Indians with liquor for husking corn for him.

That evening, the Indians sat around a campfire drinking. They became drunk and got a little carried away. They hollered and shot their guns. This enthusiasm startled the settlers, who were already on edge from the increased tensions. They demanded that something be done to take care of this "threat." Ensign Smit sent out a group of men to investigate under orders not to engage with the Indians. Among them were Sergeant Lourensen, Jacob Jansen Stoll, six other inhabitants and six soldiers. The party came upon the four drunken Indians huddled around the campfire. Without provocation, the posse attacked. They shot one Indian in the head and captured another. They shot wildly at the third, shredding his clothes, and grabbed him. As they argued about what to do with him, he escaped. They struck the fourth, who had been lying on the ground, in the head with a sword. He jumped up and ran away. The party quickly returned to the stockade.

The next day, Stoll and Chambers, with a security escort of soldiers and civilians, went to the river to send a letter to Stuyvesant documenting the previous night's events. While returning to the stockade, the Indians ambushed them. They killed one man immediately and took thirteen prisoners. The Indians demanded and received a ransom for the prisoners but decided to torture and kill seven of them anyway.

Four to six hundred armed warriors surrounded the stockade and began a two-and-a-half-week siege. During this time, they shot fire arrows into the stockade, burning some grain stacks and a barn. They slaughtered at least fourteen horses and several cows that lived outside the fort. Finally, on the night of October 8, the siege ended after a long series of continuous attacks and many Indian casualties. The settlers suffered only one casualty: Jan, the son of Cornelis Barentsen Slecht.[4]

Word of the siege reached Stuyvesant in New Amsterdam. He recruited about 190 soldiers, both voluntary and involuntary, and arrived at Esopus on October 10. Since the siege had already ended, there was no longer a need for reinforcements. Stuyvesant returned with his troops to New Amsterdam.

Over the rest of the fall and winter, things remained a strained stalemate. Both sides waited for the best opportunity to take action, and neither side wanted to give in. On March 17, 1660, a patrol of forty soldiers, led by Ensign Smit, came upon a settlement of about sixty Indians not far from the stockade. They attacked the group, killing three or four, capturing fourteen and burning the wigwams. They put twelve of the captives on a boat to New Amsterdam the next day.

Skirmishes continued without success for either side. On May 25, 1660, Stuyvesant and the council, in an attempt to scare the Esopus and show them the power of the Dutch, sent ten of the Indian captives from New Amsterdam to the Dutch island of Curacao in the Caribbean. They joined the African slaves under the control of the Dutch West India Company. This act did not create the desired effect, and the hostilities continued.

Premaeker, the Great Sachem

At the end of May, Ensign Smit and seventy-five men went out with an Indian prisoner/guide and came to a spot where they could see a group of Indians across a swollen river. They also saw the oldest and greatest of the Esopus sachems, Premaeker, fishing from a canoe. Smit and his men retreated unseen and regrouped. The guide took them on another route to the other side of the stream. Smit and his men arrived at the settlement. Smit wrote:

> [The Indians] *discovered us through the barking of their dogs and fled quietly into the woods, without a shot having been fired by us or by them and we got only one gun in the house and while looking for a canoe to cross over the Kill, we found the canoe, in which the old Premaeker had fished: this Premaeker is the oldest Sachem of the Aesopus savages and father to our prisoner* [guide] *Dosquartas. As he was a very old man and spoke in arrogant words to our men, saying "What are you doing here, you dogs" and aimed his gun at us, we took away his gun and six knives and a hatchet and as it was a great distance we could not take him along and therefore gave him a whack with his own hatchet.*[5]

Smit's men took Premaeker's canoe, crossed the kill and headed home. A group of Indians ambushed them, jumping out of bushes and wounding one soldier. The Indians retreated as quickly as they had come, and Smit's men returned to the stockade without another incident.

In a boundary description dated April 2, 1670, Premaeker's Land is described as

> *a tract of river lowlands situated on the northwest side of the Esopus Creek, and running southwestward from near the mouth of what was later known as Preymaker's Creek. This creek is mentioned in the 1687 boundary description of the Kingston Commons. The stream flows out*

Premaeker Falls on Hurley Mountain Road is known locally by many different names. In 1900, it was called Vollicher Falls. *Courtesy of the Hurley Museum.*

> *from Binnewater Lake in the Town of Kingston, about half a mile east of the eastern tip of the Ashokan Reservoir. It turns a south-southwesterly direction crossing into the Town of Hurley, then bends southeasterly and joins another stream at the edge of the flats at the edge of the Esopus Creek, into which they combine. It is believed the old sachem lived near the mouth of the stream and so given his name to the Kill and land.*[6]

Treaty and Peace

A younger, more active sachem, Seuwackenamo, had been traveling in the northern New Jersey area when Premaeker was murdered. He was working with other tribes, trying to convince the Dutch authorities that the Esopus Indians desired peace. He finally succeeded and, along with Stuyvesant and the others from Fort Amsterdam, forged a treaty on July 15, 1660, at the stockade. Many historians believe that the site of the signing was in the area of the Academy Green, in Kingston, at the intersection of Albany and Clinton Avenues.[7]

The treaty defined the terms of peace and how to deal with individual incidents in order to avoid another outbreak of war. The Esopus were required to pay five hundred *schepels* (bushels) of maize to replace the ransom that they had received for the settler captives they had not returned. They also had to give the Dutch authorities the lowlands of both sides of the Esopus Creek for a distance of two or three (Dutch) miles. This area covered the land in present-day Hurley and into Marbletown. The Dutch returned three of the Indians from Curacao but held the rest as a carrot to encourage peaceful behavior from the Indians.[8]

For the next three years, there was peace. More settlers arrived, and they enlarged the stockade. On May 16, 1661, Stuyvesant set up a government for Esopus. He changed the name from Esopus to *Wildwyck*, from the Dutch loosely meaning "wild or Indian district or region."

Stuyvesant and the Council of New Netherlands at New Amsterdam appointed Roelof Swartwout as *schout*. A *schout* acted as a judge in civil matters and as prosecutor in minor criminal offenses. Swartwout held the position until the middle of 1664. Evert Pels, Cornelis Barentsen Slecht and Aldert Heymans Roosa were appointed *scheppens*, or commissioners. This board of magistrates only had legal powers in Wildwyck. Each year, new commissioners were appointed

In order to provide religious services to the people of Wildwyck, Dominie Hermanus Bloom arrived from Fort Orange to become the permanent pastor. In 1661, Stuyvesant created a tax on farmland and house lots and an excise tax on liquor to pay for the construction of the minister's house. This building was also used for religious services and court matters.[9]

NIEUW DORP: THE "NEW VILLAGE"

On April 6, 1662, Philip Pietersen Schuyler and several other Beverwyck businessmen petitioned director and governor Stuyvesant to create a new village. The petition read as follows:

> *To the Noble, Worshipful, his Honor the Director-General and the Honorable Council of New Netherland*

Show with all respect Philipp Pietersen Schuyler, Volekert Jansen and Goosen Gerritsen van Schaick, together with Jan Thomas and Andries Herbertsen, inhabitants of the village of Beverwyck near Fort Orange, that it is evident that the prosperity of this province of New Netherland rests principally on agriculture and commerce; therefore the petitioners are very desirous to establish with many more people a new village at the Great Esopus, where a great deal of uncultivated land lies and the petitioners and other people are very willing and resolved, to begin farming in earnest and continue in it; they address themselves therefore to your Honble Worships with their humble request, that your Honble Worships will please for the benefit of the province to order a survey for a new village and farmlands on the Great Esopus, in the most convenient locality, which may be found and to have it laid out in as many lots as the area of the land may admit and whereas the abovenamed petitioners are the first undertakers and settlers, to enter upon and cultivate the aforesaid lands on the Esopus, they respectfully request, that your Honble Worships will please to give and grant to each of them forty or fifty morgens of land, at and near the spot, where the new village on the Esopus shall be laid out: the petitioners promise, each for himself, to enter upon their allotted lands immediately, to fence, plough, sow it, to build on the lots in the village houses, barns etc and to furnish the cattle, necessary for such bouweries; that the petitioners may also receive title-deeds in debita forma for the lands and house lots, which doing etc they remain.

Your Honble Worships Very obedient servants

Philipp Pietersen Schuyler
Volkert Jansen
Goosen Gerritsen Van Schaick
Andries Herbertsen
Jan Thomas

The petition was granted, and on May 4, leases were created for the tenant farms. In addition to the petitioners, lots were granted to inhabitants of Wildwyck, including Louis du Bois, Antoine Crispell and Aldert Hetmans Roosa. The tenants lived rent-free for the first year. The landowners had to provide all of the wood needed to build the houses, barns, fences and anything else necessary for the farms' operation. They

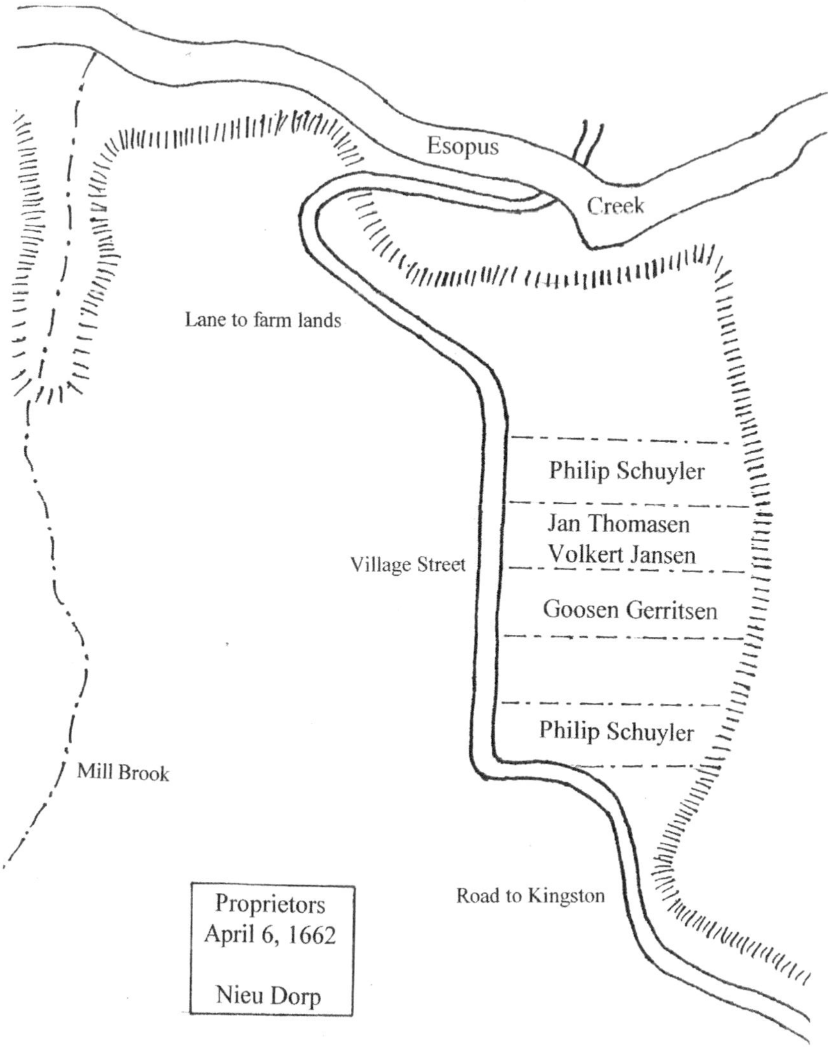

Diagrams of the original Nieuw Dorp show the proprietors of the original properties and the tenant farmers who occupied and worked the property. In some cases, they were the same person. *Courtesy of David Baker.*

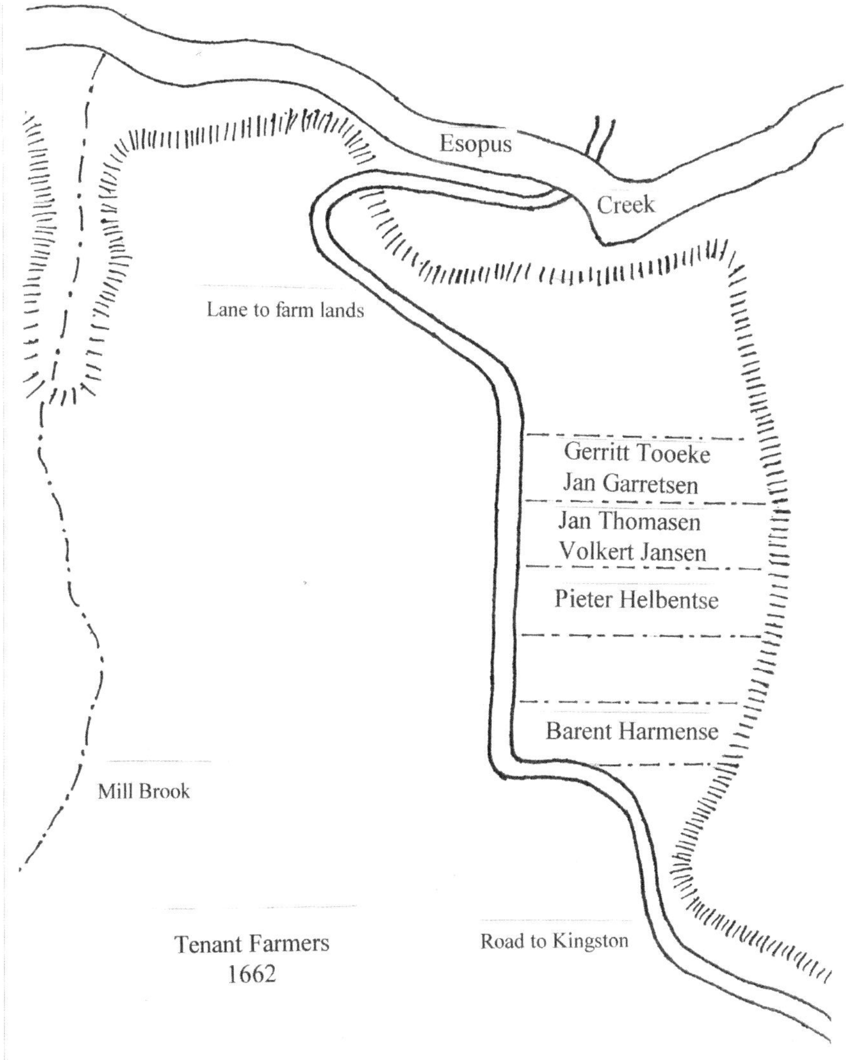
Esopus
Creek
Lane to farm lands
Gerritt Tooeke
Jan Garretsen
Jan Thomasen
Volkert Jansen
Pieter Helbentse
Barent Harmense
Mill Brook
Road to Kingston
Tenant Farmers
1662

also had to provide animals, plows and a cart and to build a bridge across the Esopus Creek. The tenants leased the land for four years, and many purchased the land when the lease was up, as shown in the 1667 records:

April 13	Nicholas Varlet and Thomas Hall	two lots at Hurley
April 15	Nicholas Varlett and Co.	land
April 15	Thomas Hall and Co.	ten acres
April 23	Lambert Huyberts Brink	sixty-eight acres
April 25	Goosen Gerrites	sixty-six acres and a lot
April 25	Philipp Pietersen Schuyler,	land
April 29	Jan Tommassen	sixty-six acres
May 2	Jan Violckert	forty-eight acres
May 7	Louis du Bois	forty acres
June	Cornelius Wynkoop	twenty-four acres
June 17	Anthony Crispell	sixteen acres
June 18	Matthew Blanchan	lot
June 28	Cornelius Wynkoop	land
July 23	Roelof Swartwout	land
August 5	Lambert Huyberts Brink	eighteen acres at Hurley

These were just the first of many land purchases. The Hurley properties were all quickly bought. Soon, settlers moved up the Esopus Creek to what is now Marbletown and, within a year or two, claimed the lands now known as Rochester and Wawarsing. It was soon discovered that the surveys were not as accurate as was originally thought, and some lands were owned by more than one party.

In 1669, Governor Francis Lovelace appointed a commission to resolve all disputed land matters.[10]

The Second Esopus War

Settling in an untouched frontier has its own challenges, but when strangers move into an area and take over the land you have been farming for centuries, this can create resentment. Relations between the Esopus Indians and the settlers had remained amicable since the First Esopus War. History shows that the Esopus held a grudge against the settlers regarding the treaty of 1660. Their biggest complaint seems to have been a discrepancy over which lowlands of the Esopus Creek had been agreed upon previously. The Indians felt that Stuyvesant took more land than was agreed upon and they wanted more compensation. They also wanted their captured brothers to be returned. The Dutch were becoming increasingly concerned about the increased sale to and consumption of liquor by the Indians. Stuyvesant reminded the settlers that this was the problem that had started the First Esopus War. A fourth factor causing unrest involved the reputation of the Esopus Indians among the other tribes. The Mohawks had become allies with the Dutch, and they referred to the Esopus as an inferior tribe.

Many believe that the latter was the most influential factor in driving the Esopus Indians to plan a coordinated attack on Wildwyck and the new village, despite Stuyvesant's promise to visit and deliver gifts to encourage the peace. On June 7, just after eleven in the morning, they attacked and burned the two settlements. A letter from the board of magistrates to Stuyvesant and the Council describes the events of the massacre at Esopus:

> *The Court at Wildwyck to the Council of New Netherland:*
>
> *Right Honorable, most respected, wise, prudent and very discreet Lords.*
>
> *We, your Honors' very faithful subjects have to report, pursuant to the order of the Right Honorable Heir Director General, in the form a Journal, that in obedience to his Honors' order, received on the 30th of May last, we caused the Indian Sachems to be notified on the 5th of June to be prepared to expect the arrival of the Right Honorable Heir Director General, to receive the promised presents, and to renew the peace. This notification was communicated to them through Capt. Thomas Chambers, to which they answered: "If peace were to be renewed with them, the Honorable Heir Director General should, with some unarmed persons, sit with them in the open field, without the gate, as it was their own custom to meet unarmed when receiving peace or in other negotiations."*

But they, unmindful of the preceding statement, surprised and attacked us between the hours of 11 and 12 o'clock in the forenoon on Thursday the 7th instant Entering in bands through all the gates, they divided and scattered themselves among all the houses and dwellings in a friendly manner, having with them a little maize and a few beans to sell to our Inhabitants, but which means they kept them in their houses, and thus went from place to place as spies to discover our strength in men. And after they been about a short quarter of an hour within this place, some people on horseback rushed in the Mill gate from the New Village crying out "The Indians have destroyed the New Village!"

And with these words, the Indians here in this village immediately fired a shot and made a general attack on our village from the rear, murdering our people in their homes with their axes and tomahawks, and firing on them with guns and pistols; they seized whatever women and children they could catch and carried them prisoners outside the gates, plundered the houses and set the village on fire to windward, it blowing at the time from the south. The remaining Indians commanded all the streets, firing from the corner houses which they occupied and through the curtains outside along the highways, so that some of our Inhabitants, on their way to their houses to get arms, were wounded and slain. When the flames were at their height, the wind changed to the west, were it not for which the fire would have been much more destructive.

So rapidly and silently did Murder do his work that those in different parts of the village were not aware of it until those who had been wounded happened to meet each other, in which way most of the others also had warning. The greater portion of our men were abroad at their field labors, and but few in the village. Near the mill gate were Albert Gysbertsen with two servants, and Tireck Claesen de Wit, at the Sheriff's, himself with two carpenters two clerks and one thresher, at Cornelius Barentsen Slecht's, himself and his son; at the Domonie's, himself and two carpenters and one laboring man; at the guard house, a few soldiers; at the gate towards the river, Henderick Jochemsen and Jacob, the Brewer, but Henderick Jochamsen was very seriously wounded in his house by two shots at an early hour.

But these aforesaid men, most of whom had neither guns nor side arms, were the Indians, through God's mercy, chased and put to flight on the alarm being given by the Sheriff. Capt. Thomas Chambers was wounded on coming in from without, issued immediate orders (with the Sheriff and Commissioners) to secure the gates; to clear the gun and to drive out the

Savages, who were still about a half an hour in the village aiming at their persons, which was accordingly done. The burning of the houses, the murder and carrying off of women and children is here omitted, as there have already been communicated to your Honors the 10th June. After these few men had been collected against the Barbarians, by degrees the others arrived who, it has been stated, were abroad at their field labors, and we found ourselves when ministered in the evening, including those from the new village, who took refuge amongst us, in number 69 efficient men, both qualified and unqualified. The burnt palisades were immediately replaced by new tones, and the people distributed, during the night, along the bastions and curtains to keep watch.

On the 10th, 10 horsemen were commanded to ride down to the Redoubt (Rondout) and to examine its condition. They returned with wood that the soldiers at the Redoubt had not seen any Indians. They brought also with them the Sergeant, who had gone the preceding morning to the Redoubt, and as he heard of his return of the mischief committed by the Indians in the village, he went back up the Redoubt and stayed there. In addition to the Sergeant, they brought the man who had fled from the new village.

On the 16th, towards evening, Sergeant Christian Nessen went with a troop of soldiers, sent us by your Honors, being 42 men, and three wagons, to the Redoubt, with letters for the Manhatans, addressed to your Honors, and to bring up ammunition from the Redoubt. On their return, the Indians made an attempt, at the first hill, to take the ammunition from these troops. The Sergeant, having divided his men into separate bodies, evinced great courage against the Indians, skirmishing with them from the first, to past the second hill, and defending the wagons so well that they arrived in safety in the village. He had, however, one killed and six wounded. The dead man was brought in next morning, having been stripped naked, and having had his right hand cut off by the Indians. Some of the reinforcement of horse and foot was immediately ordered out, but before they arrived the Indians had been put to flight by the above named Sergeant.

This, Right Honorable Lords, is what we have deemed necessary to communicate to you in the form of a journal as to how and in what manner the Indians have acted toward us and we towards them in the preceding circumstances. As we humbly and respectfully request your Honors to be pleased to send us hither for the wounded by the earliest opportunity, some prunes and linen with some wine to strengthen them, and whatever else not obtainable here your Honors may think proper, also, carabines, cutlasses, and gun flints, and we request that the carabines may be Snapaume, as the people here are but little conversant with the use of the aquabus (ver roe), also some spurs for the horsemen. In addition to this, also, some reinforcements in men, inasmuch as harvest will commence in about 14 days from date. Herewith ending, we commend your Honors to God's fatherly care and protection. Done, Wildwyck, this 20th June 1663.

ROELOF SWARTWOUT,
The mark of ALBERT GYSBERTSEN,
TIERECK CLASSEN DE WITT,
THOMAS CHAMBERS,
GYSBERT VAN IMBROCH,
CHRISTIAEN NYSSEN,
HENDRICK JOCHEMSEN[11]

KILLED AT WILDWYCK

Jan Alberts in front of his house
Thomas Chambers' negro on the farm
Lechten Ditteck on the farm
Barent Garretsen in front of his house
Willem Jansen Hap in Pieter van Hael's house
Hendrick Jansen Looman on the farm
Hey Olferts in the gunner's house
Willem Jansen Seba opposite his door
Jan the Smith in his house

SOLDIERS

Christiaen Andriesen in the street
Dominicus in Jan Albert's house
Handrick Martensen on the farm

WOMEN AND CHILDREN

Jan Albertsen's wife, big with child and daughter in front of their house
Mattys Capito's wife killed and burned in her house
Pieter van Hael's wife, shot and burnt in her house
Willem Hep's child burnt alive in the house
Lichten Dirreck's wife burnt, with her lost fruit, behind Barent Gerritsen's house

Wounded

Andries Barents shot in front of his house
Thomas Chambers shot in the woods
Albert Gerretsen shot in front of his house
Hendrick Jachemsen shot in his house
Michiel Ferre shot in front of his house, died of his wounds on June 18
Jan du Parck shot in the house of Arient Pietersen Tack
Paulus, the Nooeman shot in the street
Hendrick, the Director General's servant shot in the street in front of Aert Jacobsen

Taken Prisoner

Femmetje, sister of Hilletje, being recently married to Joost Ariens
Master Gysbert's wife
Hester Douwe and her daughter Sara
Tjerck Claessen de Witt's oldest daughter (Tjaatje)
Domone Laer's wife and child
Ariaen Garritsen's daughter
Mattys Roloffseniel's two little boys

Houses Burnt

Of Jacob Boerhams (2)	*Hans Carolusen (1)*	*Lichten Dirrick (1)*
Michiel Farre (1)	*Albert Gerritsen (1)*	*Barent Garretsen (2)*
Willem Hap (1)	*Mattys (1)*	*Mattys Roloffsen (1)*
Pieter van Hael (1)		

Killed in the New Village

Derrick Ariaensen shot on his horse
Jacques Tyssen beside Barent's house
Harmensen found dead and stript naked behind the wagon

Taken Prisoner

Jan Gerritsen on Volckert's bouwery
Of Mattys Blanchan two children
Jan Barents wife and child
Antone Crupel wife and child (Maria M.)
Louwis du Bois wife and three children
Michiel Farre two children
Marten Harmensen wife and four children

Barent Harmensen wife and child
Lambert Hybertsen (Brink) wife and three children
Aldert Heymans two children
Henderick Jochems child
Grietje Westercamp wife and three children

The new village is entirely destroyed except a new uncovered barn, one rick and a little stack of reed.[12]

This was not a one-time attack. The settlers, besieged in the stockade, were on constant lookout. Anyone needing to go outside the walls had a military escort. Skirmishes continued between the soldiers and Indians. On June 30, the Dutch West India Company appointed Martin Cregier, a burgomaster of New Amsterdam, as captain lieutenant of the military forces under Stuyvesant. He and his soldiers arrived at Esopus in July. During his six months at Esopus, Cregier kept a detailed daily journal of his men's actions and the eventual return of the captives.[13] The war continued until winter.

THE ENGLISH COME

On September 4, 1664, Wildwyck prepared for a possible attack by the English ships sailing up the Hudson River. Stuyvesant and the Dutch surrendered to the English on September 8. The English renamed New Amsterdam, New York; and Fort Orange, Fort Albany. Richard Nicolls became the governor of New York. On October 7, 1665, the Esopus Indians and Governor Nicolls signed a treaty reaffirming the terms of the previous treaty that the Esopus held with the Dutch.

It did not take long before the Dutch settlers began to worry less about the Indians and more about the occupying English soldiers. One notable clash, known as the Esopus Mutiny, occurred on February 4, 1667. It was reported that the English military commander Captain Daniel Brodhead, appointed on September 14, 1665, repeatedly cut, beat and wounded Cornelis Barentsen Slecht, a sergeant in the civilian militia, in his own home. Five English soldiers arrived at the house to find Brodhead's face scratched and his uniform torn. They hauled Slecht away to prison. Hearing the cries of Slecht's wife and children, a group of between five and nine men went to the magistrates for guidance. Soon, there were fifty to seventy armed men demanding Slecht's release.

The Wildwyck magistrates appealed to Brodhead to release Slecht so that he could face a proper legal proceeding. Brodhead refused, saying that he would hold him as long as he wanted, and he practically dared the people to try to come and get Slecht out. Brodhead and seven soldiers came out to meet the mob. There followed a lot of shouting and threatening. Lieutenant Thomas Chambers ordered the mob members to return to their homes, but they didn't listen. Later that night, the group finally disbanded.

Other complaints claimed that Captain Broadhead had beaten Tierck Clausen and put him in prison without justification. Broadhead had also allegedly demanded free brandy from Louis du Bois. Du Bois had refused, demanding payment, and in response, Broadhead threw an anker of brandy on the ground. Many more accusations of threats and violence were brought against Broadhead and his soldiers.

From April 25 to 27, a special court was held to hear complaints from both sides. Because of the hearings, Antoine Dalva, Cornelis Barentsen Slecht and Aldert Heymans Roosa and his son, Arient Aldertsen Roosa, were found guilty of inciting a rebellious and mutinous act. They were imprisoned. Captain Brodhead was relieved of his duties and died not long after the incident.[14]

On April 6, 1668, Governor Nicolls moved the English garrison out of Wildwyck to an area near the present Marbletown-Hurley line, near the Washmaker lands.

In August 1668, Frances Lovelace succeeded Nicolls as governor. He came to Esopus in September to evaluate the plans for the "Further New Dorp" (Marbletown) and to hear and evaluate claims of those who had received land of the "Nearer New Dorp" (Hurley) in 1662–63.[15] Few settlers had returned to Nieuw Dorp to rebuild their homes. Many soon returned under the threat of forfeiture of the land.

A special commission, made up of Thomas Chambers, Schout William Beekman, Christopher Berisford, Henry Pawling and two military representatives, was appointed on September 11 to settle various affairs. On September 17, it renamed Nieuw Dorp and Further Nieuw Dorp Hurley and Marbleton, respectively, and on the September 25, the Esopus/Wildwyck area was renamed Kingston. Kingston and Hurley are both believed to have been named after Lovelace's ancestral home in Berkshire, England.[16]

There was a small area between Hurley and Marbletown known as the Half-Way Ground. On September 21, 1669, Governor Lovelace granted Robert Goldsberry permission to build a house there. This grant was received on April 8, 1670. The house was to serve as a rest stop for travelers between the two villages. Some consider this a lost village because little else is known of its history, and there is little documentation available, except for those first references by Lovelace and the commission for its creation. The Half-Way Ground is located in the area between Route 209, the Esopus Creek, Creekside Drive and Old Route 209.[17]

The commission also created the governing bodies for the towns. Christopher Biersford became chief magistrate of Hurley and Marbleton, in charge of keeping the peace between the towns. Under him were two resident overseers from their respective towns. Louis du Bois and Aldert Heymans Roosa became overseers for Hurley. They were also in charge of the maintenance of the highways and roads. Thomas Chambers became surveyor general of all highways and common roads and had ultimate authority over the three towns. Henry Pawling became the officer in charge of Indian affairs.[18] The commission completed its work and was dissolved on September 29.

By the spring of 1670, all of the landowners had returned to rebuild Hurley, as mentioned earlier. On January 24, 1670, Tjreck Claesen de Witt was granted permission to construct a house, barn and outbuildings on his land midway between Kingston and Hurley. Though not fully determined from the records, Marc Fried, author of *The Early History of Kingston and Uldter County*, states that he believes a house was erected by 1673, though it is not determined if it is the stone house that stands today off Hurley Avenue or if the original was a wooden one. The house remained in the family until 1875.

A new commission was formed, made up of the same four men, and their biggest job was to divide the land given to the soldiers. They also created a militia for Hurley composed of all the adult male residents of Hurley and Marbletown. They appointed Henry Pawling as captain, Christopher Biersford as lieutenant and Aldert Heymans Roosa as sergeant.

In 1671, the Duke's Laws established a justice of the peace and a court of sessions.[19]

On May 2, 1671, Thomas Delaval and Captain Dudley Lovelace arrived in Kingston as special commissioners. They sparked some political upheaval, which was later resolved. In July 1673, the Dutch retook New York. Town

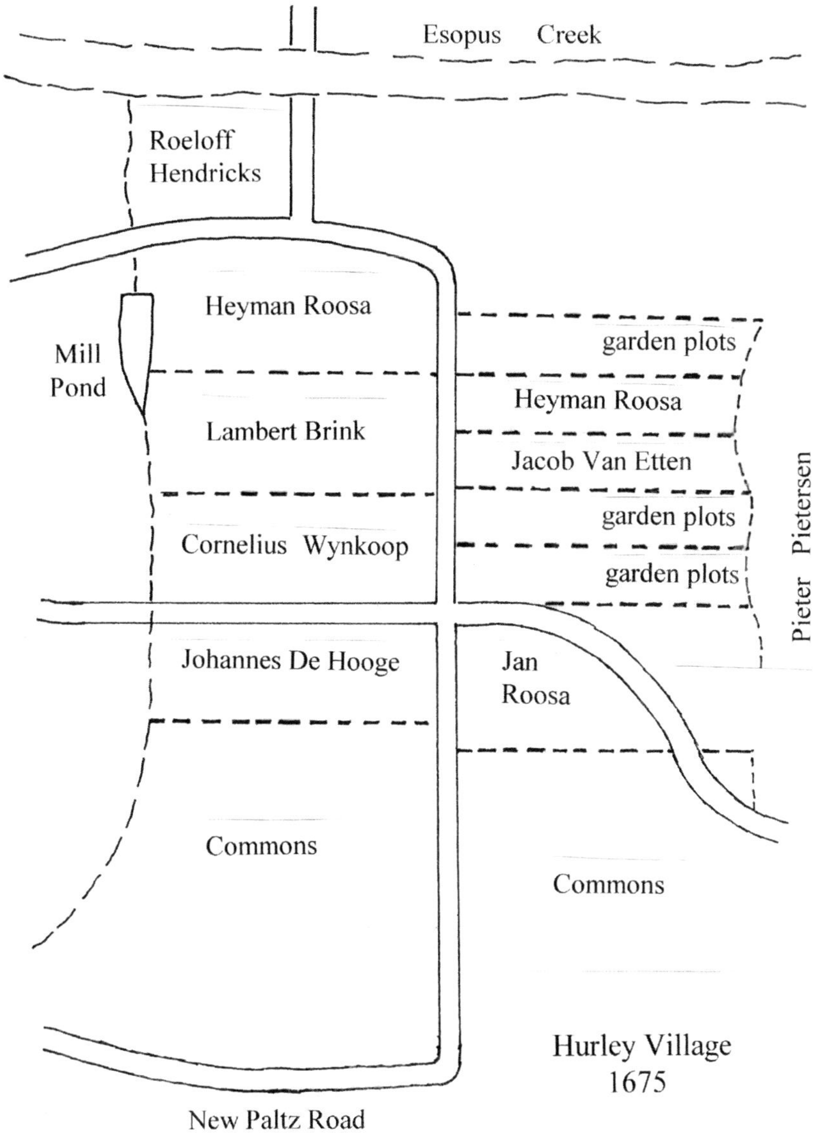

An illustrative map of Hurley's Main Street in 1675. This is the best guess of the location of the landowners and layout at this time. *Courtesy of David Baker.*

names changed again—New York City became New Orange, Fort Albany became Fort Nassau, Kingston became Swaenenburgh and New York reverted to New Netherland. By February of the following year, the area had returned to English hands, and the names changed back.

New Paltz Patent

Led by Louis du Bois, twelve Huguenots, referred to as the *Duzine*, negotiated with the Esopus Indians to purchase land in the Wallkill Valley. The meeting was held in du Bois' store in Nieuw Dorp. The Huguenots had admired the beauty and fertility of the land when they traversed it with Captain Creiger's forces searching for their captured family members. Governor Edmund Andros approved the license to negotiate the purchase in April 1677. The license included about ninety-two thousand acres encompassing 144 square miles of the current town of Lloyd and parts of Esopus, New Paltz and Rosendale. They finalized an agreement on May 26, and the Indians issued a final signed agreement in September. In 1709, Surveyor General Grahm surveyed the land. An excerpt of the agreement reads as follows:

> *THE ARTICLE OF AGREEMENT*
>
> *To-day, the 26th of May in the year 1677, an agreement was made by the below-named parties, pursuant to a license from the Honable Governor Edmund Andras, dated the 28th of April 1677, with the undersigned Esopus Indians concerning the purchase of a certain tract of land on the other side of the Rondout Kill.*[20]
>
> *Beginning at the high hill called Masgaaeck, thence Southeast toward the Great River to the point called J.*
>
> *The Indians shall also have fully as much liberty and license to hunt all kind of wild animal and to fish, as the Christians. This land the Indians have engaged to sell for the goods here specified below:*
>
> *40 Kettles, 10 large 20 small, 100 knives, 40 axes, 4 ankers of wine, 40 addices, 40 guns, 40 shirts, 60 duffels coats, 100 fathoms of white wampum, 60 blankets, 300 fathom of black wampum, 100 nails, 60 pairs of socks, one half of them small ones, 1 schepel of pipes, 1 keg of powder, wine has been given for the horses.*

The parties of either part herewith acknowledge to have agreed and have signed this with their hands.

Lowis Du Boys, Christian de Yoo, Abraham Hasbroock, Andries Lefebre

The rest of the patentees were Jean Hasbrouck, Peter Deyo, Leurens Bevier, Anthony Crispell, Abraham du Bois, Hugo Freer, Isaac du Bois and Symeon LeFevre. All of these men, except for Anthony Crispell, built homes on the new land.

On September 30, 1682, Thomas Dongan was commissioned as governor of New York. He arrived in New York in August 1683 with instructions from the Duke of York for governing. This included permission to create a popularly elected general assembly. Elections were held, and the first general assembly convened. On February 6, 1658, King Charles II died, and the duke became James II of England and James VII of Scotland. Upon hearing this news, Dongan prorogued the general assembly. Soon after, James II abolished the assembly and all popular elections.[21] Dongan left office amid turmoil and various accusations in August 1689.

1689 Pledge of the People of Hurley to Support Their Representatives

We the undersigned hereby acknowledge to agree to what our committee may do or enact for the welfare and allegiance of our Gracious Majesty King William and Queen Mary for the benefit of our country and the advancement of the Protestant Religion, whereunto we pledge both our body and our lives. In witness of the Truth we have subscribed these with our own hands.
The 12 December 1689, at Hurley

Hendrick Clasen
Johannes d'Hooges
Roelof Hendrix
Adrian Garritsen
Hendrick
mark of Gerrit Cornelius
mark of Tho. Swartwout

Matys Blansjan
mark of Cornelius Gerrits
Anthony Crispe
mark of Pieter Pietersen
Hybert Lambertsen
Jan Elcings
Barent Kunst
mark of Jacob Gerritsen
Luer Jacobsen
Mark of Hants van Etcen
Mattys Sleght van Kingston
Johanes Juriansen van Kingston
Agrees with the original Wm. Montagne

EARLY HOUSES OF HURLEY

Bevier House
Main Street

The original house was a smaller one-room cottage, built on the foundation of a wooden house believed to have been burned in the Second Esopus War. In 1711–12, Ary Roosa purchased the property. The stone cottage, built by 1720, had an end-wall jambless fireplace. The house is built on the original town lots four, five and six. Lot six is now the Route 209 bridge. A second three-walled addition with a jambless fireplace was added about 1730, creating a duplex. Lucas Elmendorf (1718–1795), son of Coenradt Elmendorf and Blandina Kiersted, purchased the property in June 1752.[22] The stone kitchen was added before the Revolution. During the Revolution, Lucas ran a cooperage and supplied grain-shipping barrels to local farmers and to the war effort. He also served as a sergeant in the First Ulster Foot Regiment. Lucas married Catherina Wynkoop (1722–1756?), daughter of Colonel Cornelius Wynkoop and Hendrika Newkirk, in 1747. She soon became ill and needed constant care. Her sister Lea (1728–?) moved in to care for her. After Catherina died, Lea continued living in her own section of the house. Two domestic

The Bevier House, circa 2007. Part of the property was taken when the railroad access was dug and the bridge was built. *Author's collection.*

slaves, Sarie and Lane, helped run the house. Lea remained in the house until at least 1800.

Judge Lucas Elmendorf, nephew of Lucas and son of Jonathan Elmendorf and Magdelena Smeedes, inherited the house, but he apparently never lived there. Lucas was married to Ann Waddell of New York City. The house went to his son William Henry Elmendorf (1798–?).

Richard M. Bevier and his wife, Garetle, purchased the house in 1887. The house, as it stands today, was fully constructed by the mid-1800s.

Brink House
Wynkoop Road

In 1670, Lambert Huybertse built this stone house on the property he purchased in 1667. The original house was a one-room cottage with a brick addition built about 1840. A brick façade was added over the stone so that it would match. The stone kitchen was added in 1740. Little

The Brink House about 1900. Since it lies on the lowlands near the Hurley Mountain, the property—and nearby Brinks Lane—is susceptible to flooding. *Courtesy of the Hurley Museum.*

remains of the original structure, except for the exterior walls. The house remained in the Brink family until Sarah Brink Dietz, daughter of William Brink, sold it in 1958.

Du Bois Cottage
Old Route 209

This house sits on part of the original land patent to Louis du Bois, dating back to the 1660s. There are two houses on the original patent, and it is not known which is older. The original Marbletown Road followed along the Esopus Creek. In 1709, the Queens Highway was created, replacing the Marbletown Road. It is now known as Old Route 209. The location of the cottage on the Queens Highway dates to after 1709. The original wooden house mat have sat closer to the creek.

This house was first a wood structure with a three-walled stone addition that dates to about 1735. It appears to be a two-room house with an entrance—the first of this style in Hurley. The house remained in the du Bois family until the mid-1900s.

The du Bois Cottage on Old Route 209, circa 2001. *Courtesy of David Baker.*

Elmendorf House and Half Moon Tavern
Main Street

This property was part of a larger parcel owned by Jan Alderts Roosa. The original one-room stone cottage dates back to about 1690. Jan sold the property to his son Aldert Janse about the time of his marriage to Rebecca Schepmoes. Aldert died before 1744, and the house passed to his sons, Dirck (1715–1797) and either Jan A. or Abraham. They sold the house to Wilhelmus Elmendorf in 1749. Elmendorf was a weaver and built the large east wing as his commercial weaving room. He established the Half Moon Inn. When he died in 1754, heavily in debt, his widow and children ran the tavern.

In the late 1700s, Petrus Elmendorf, who lived across the street, was the tavern keeper for the Half Moon Tavern.

In the early 1800s, Petrus bought the property and ran a dairy farm until 1950. He also accumulated several farm lots in the town.

In the late 1800s, John L. Elmendorf used the Loom House in the backyard to make axe handles. His wife, Catherine Hasbrock Elmendorf, made rugs on the second floor.

The Elmendorf House and Half Moon Tavern, circa 1900. *Courtesy of the Hurley Museum.*

In the 1920s, the east end was a general store, and a corner of the building became the U.S. Post Office when Peter Elmendorf became postmaster. It remained until the 1930s.

The black walnut tree is about one hundred years old.

HONORABLE LUCAS ELMENDORF (1761–1843) was the son of Colonel Jonathan Elmendorf. He graduated from Princeton in 1782 and was admitted to the bar three years later. He was elected to Congress in 1797, 1799 and 1801. He was Ulster County district attorney from 1801 to 1811. He married Ann Waddell in New York City in 1797, and they had three children. He also served on the New York Assembly, in the 1801 Continental Congress and in the New York Senate and was appointed to the Board of Regents of the University of New York. In 1815, he became a justice of the Ulster County Court of Common Pleas.

Though he may have never lived in Hurley, part of Lucas will always be here. In 1805, turnpikes were being built everywhere. The New York State legislature passed a bill creating roads from the Hudson River communities to the rural ones to the west. Lucas invested $40,000 of his personal money into the Neversink Turnpike Road Company. He became a member of the board of directors and was appointed manager of road construction. Surveys were made for the new Lucas Turnpike, which led from Kingston through Hurley, Marbletown, Rochester and Wawarsing and through Sullivan and Delaware Counties to Cochecton, in Broome

County. The road was never completed, though present-day U.S. Route 209 follows a similar route.

Lucas was also notorious for keeping a land case in the legal system for fifty-two years.

Children:
William Henry (1798–?)
Juliana (1800–?)
Annetie Magdalena (1803–?)

The Abe Houghtaling House
Corner of Main Street and Hurley Avenue

In 1699, Pieter Pietersen Ostrander and his wife, Rebecca, purchased this two-acre property from Anthony Crispell. This is the first record of an Ostrander purchasing property in Hurley. This house began as a single-room cottage that faced Main Street. When Hurley Avenue was built about 1708, an addition was built on the new street side, and the roofline was rotated ninety degrees.

The Houghtaling House, circa 1900. *Courtesy of the Hurley Museum.*

In 1715, the house and property were either deeded or sold to the Ostranders' son, Arent. Later, before the Revolution, the stone kitchen was added. During the Revolution, the house served as a tavern. Local stories claim that George Washington stopped here during his visit to Hurley in 1782. In 1780, the property was owned by Huybert Ostrander. Abe Houghtaling owned the property during the mid-1800s and added the store section to the far left of the house, where he had his shop as a successful wagon maker.

Patentee Manor
Old Route 209

This house is situated on a 1720 land grant. The original building is a 1696 stone cottage, built by Cornelius Kool (also spelled Cool). In 1745, it was converted into a two-story Georgian mansion. In 1708, King George granted a patent of land extending from Woodstock to New Paltz and included five neighboring towns. It was called the Hurley Patent, from which the Cornelius Cool family greatly benefitted. One hundred years later, the lands

The Patentee Manor home of the Patentee Lighting Company, circa 2001. *Courtesy of David Baker.*

were divided among the citizens, ending a prosperous real estate venture. The Cool family was of Dutch and English descent, and their home reflects this. Cornelius Cool married in 1694.

In 1957, owners Stephen and Carolyn Walogurski began a ten-year renovation project. They formed Hurley Patentee Lighting Company. They create lighting fixtures that replicate those found in historic colonial homes.[23]

The Schepmoes House
Hurley Avenue

The present kitchen area is the original building—a one-room cottage owned by Dirck Schepmoes in the 1680s. The original house was burned by the British during the attack on Kingston on October 16, 1777. It was the last house burned by the British as they advanced toward Hurley. Before they marched any closer, a retreat signal called them back to their

The Dirck Schepmoes House, circa 2009, on Hurley Avenue. This house is hidden to most drivers since it sits down the hill. *Author's collection.*

ships on Kingston's shores. Sometime in the 1800s, the two-story rural Georgian house was added to the old structure. In 1875, the Sagendorph family lived in the house. A rural Georgian structure has a center hall with one room on either side. The second floor is the same design as the first. Fireplaces are found on the gable walls. This design was used in rural areas to display influence and money; it has been used in the town since 1780.

The stairway to the second floor has changed from the original, as evidenced in the hall closet. The house is currently known as Pleasant View Farm.

The Ten Eyck Bowery, Henry Paul Farm
Hurley Mountain Road

The original structure began as two rooms, now the core of the present structure. It is identical to the core of the Du Mond Cottage on Main Street, including the two jambless fireplaces. This house was expanded by adding small stone additions around the core. The house was completed

The Ten Eyck Bowery, also known as the Mattys Ten Eyck House and now the Henry Paul Farm, on Hurley Mountain Road, circa 1900. *Courtesy of the Hurley Museum.*

before the Revolution. Cornelius Ten Eyck and his wife, Maria Boele, arrived from the Albany area in the 1670s and built the house before the end of the century. Their oldest son, Mattys, inherited the farm. Captain Mattys Ten Eyck married Jannetje Roosa (daughter of Aldert Heymans) in 1679, and they raised eight children. When Mattys died in 1714, his youngest son, Abraam, and Abraam's wife, Janneke Elmendorf of Kingston, along with their two children, were living on the farm with him. Abraam died in 1720, and his son Mathew and Mathew's wife, Cornelia Wynkoop, inherited the farm, where they were living.

Mathew was probably the wealthiest of the Ten Eyck family who lived on the farm. He owned extensive farmland in Esopus, growing grain. He had also purchased and continued to maintain orchards on the low hills to the east of the village. He owned two farmhouse lots for the tenants who worked the orchards. He donated land for a school in the village in 1775 and for one just south of his home in 1794.

In 1809, Mathew died, and the farm went to his youngest son, John. In 1850, the house passed to John's nephew Ten Eyck De Witt since he had no children. The homestead remained in the De Witt family until Barbara and Henry Paul purchased and restored it in 1963.

Wynkoop House
Corner of Wynkoop Road and Hurley Mountain Road

The property, containing twenty-four acres, was obtained in April 1663 by Cornelius Wynkoop. The oldest section of the house, built in stone, dates back to the late seventeenth or very early eighteenth century. A wooden section was added in the 1890s. There was an outbuilding in the horse pasture along Wynkoop Lane that housed the slaves. The property stayed in the Wynkoop family from 1663 until 1971. When Kingston was burned by the British, many refugees stayed at the home. This was home to Colonel Cornelius Wynkoop, who was killed by his slave in 1792 (described later in the book). This property was used for the farm scenes in the 1982 Sydney Pollack movie *Tootsie*.

The Wynkoop House on the corner of Hurley Mountain Road and Wynkoop Road. *Courtesy of David Baker.*

Cornelius Kool House
Old Route 209

Cornelius Kool purchased this property in 1680. There is evidence that a wooden house was built, probably shortly after the time of purchase. The original stone structure was constructed between 1705 and 1720. Kool expanded the house to its present size and then, in 1745, built the Patentee Manor next door.

The house has many great examples of seventeenth- and eighteenth-century architecture. They include large beams, wide plank floors, a steep-pitched roof, exterior fieldstone walls and evidence of leaded window frames and three jambless fireplaces. It is currently the home to Stone House Bed and Breakfast.

At this point, the foundation was laid for the new village of Hurley. Many inhabitants of Ulster County today are descendants of the original settlers of Wildwyck and Nieuw Dorp.

The Cornelius Kool (Cool) House on Old Route 209, circa 2009, has just been converted into a bed-and-breakfast. *Author's collection.*

Wagendale

The villages of Creek Locks (Wagendale) and Bloomington (Bloomendal) were at first included in the corporation of Kingston, which existed from the granting of the Kingston Patent on May 19, 1667, until 1788. Then it declined in administrative control and eventually went out of existence in 1816. When the town of Hurley was re-created on October 19, 1708, the villages of Creek Locks and Bloomington became part of that town. Then, on April 26, 1844, by an act of the New York State General Assembly, the area became part of the town of Rosendale.

The area known as Wagendale was first settled when Jacob Aertsen Van Wagenen, son of Aert Jacobsen and Annetje Gerrits Van Wagenen, purchased six hundred acres from Colonel Henry Beekman about 1682. Jacob married Matytje Low. The following were the main houses composing the hamlet of Wagendale:

Aert Aertes Van Wagenen (1679–1740) House

Aert built this house about 1699. It stands on the west side of Main Street just before the intersection of Creek Locks Road. The center part of the house was built about 1700. Additions were added later, and major renovations were probably made under the ownership of his grandson Petrus (1745–?). This house is the oldest intact structure in Rosendale. Since Jacob was living in his grandfather's house, this house went to Aert's next oldest son, Gerrit Aertse (1712–1791). Gerrit married Marytje Freer in 1736. The house appears to have remained in the family.

Yssak (Isaac) Van Wagenen (1703–1797) House

By this time, there were several houses on the Jacob Van Wagenen property. Several no longer exist. Jacob's youngest son, Isaac, married Catrina Freer. Their son, Ysaak (1729–?) married Sarah Deyo (1733–?), daughter of Henry Deyo and Margaret Wamboom. Ysaak built the sixth house in 1775. He was named one of the first deacons of the newly organized Bloomington Reformed Church in 1796. This house deteriorated and collapsed in the late 1800s.

MORE EARLY SETTLERS

ABRAHAM DELAMETER (1656–1734) married Elsie Tappen (1664–1736), daughter of Jerome Tappen, in 1693. The last name is also noted in the records as Limiter and De La Meter. He was a signer of the 1689 Oath of Allegiance.

In 1743, he purchased the village mill, house lot and milldam from Johannis Hardenburgh. The property went to his son, David Jr. and David's wife, Rebecca, and they later sold it to Cornelius Cole Jr.

Children:

Cornelius, Jacobus, David (1700–1772) and Johannis.

Abraham Jr.(1706–1776) married Rachel Low (1710–1772), daughter of Abraham Low, in 1730. They had twelve children, two of whom died young.

Triantje married Aldert Kierstede.
Janetie, Elsie's daughter, born in 1689, married William Elting.

Jacobus Conradt Moog/Elmendorf, Elmendorp (1647–before 1688) was born in Rynborch, Holland. He settled in Hurley by 1667 and married Grietje Hertse van Wagenen, daughter of Aartse Jacobsen Van Wagenen and Annetje Gerritse, in 1668.

Children:

Major Coenradt (1669–1749) married Ariaantje Gerrits van den Berg van Buren, daughter of Gerrit van den Berg, in 1693. They had four children. He then married Blandina Kierstede(1682–?), daughter of Roelof Kierstede and Eyke Roosa, in 1704. They had nine children. He served for many years in the Kingston militia. He was also a Kingston trustee for many years and served as a deacon and elder for the Kingston Reformed Church.

Geertje (1671–?) married Evert Wynkoop (1665–1746), son of Cornelis Wynkoop and Maria Longendyke, in 1688. They had six children.

Anna (dates unknown) married Matthys Jansen in 1695. They had nine children.

Jacobus (1678–?) married Aertje Cool (1689–?), daughter of Cornelius Cool and Jannetje Lambersen, in 1706. They had three children. Jacobus served as a trustee of Kingston and a deacon for the church.

Tekela (1684–?)

Major Johannes Hardenburgh (1670–before 1748) was born in New Albany. In 1689, he purchased land in Kingston. He first married Hillegonde Meijers, the daughter of Andries Meijers and Vrouwtje van der Vorst, in 1696. Both of their parents were from Holland. He then married Catherine Rutsen, daughter of Jacob Rutsen and Maria Harmen Bergen, in 1697. They had thirteen children, five of whom died young. Johannes, a successful merchant in Kingston, traded many items with the Indians. He was commissioned high sheriff of Ulster County in 1690. He served as a major in the Ulster County Militia under Colonel Rutsen. He later moved up to colonel of that regiment, but he was always referred to as "Major." In 1737, he served as a delegate in the New York Provincial Assembly and stayed there until 1745. Records report that he purchased many tracts of land, including what is known as the Great Hardenburgh Patent (discussed in chapter two).

Children:

Catherine (1696–1708)

Gerardus (1700–?) had a twin, Jacobus, who died an infant. He married Jenneken Elmendorf (1707–?), daughter of Jacobus Elmendorf (1678) and Antje Cool (1689), in 1726. He served as town supervisor from 1729 to 1738, as town clerk from 1724 to 1737 and as overseer for the middle district. They had eight children.

Martytje (1702–?) married Charles Brodhead (1696–1744), son of Charles Brodhead and Maria Ten Broeck, in 1755. The younger Charles owned twenty-seven thousand acres of land in the Great Patent. He also owned several mills, barns and other properties. He was the uncle of Charles De Wit, his sister Marie's son. They had no children.

Jacoba (1704–?) married Edward Whittaker (1704–?), son of Edward Whittaker and Hillitje Burhans, in 1729. They had five girls.

Colonel Johannes Jr. (1706–1786) married Maria du Bois (1706–1790), daughter of Louis du Bois (Jr.) and Rachel Hasbroeck, in 1728. They lived in Rosendale in the stone house built by Jacob Rutsen. They had seven children. He served on the Colonial Assembly from 1737 to 1752 and the state legislature from 1781 to 1782 and was an original trustee for Queens College, now known as Rutgers College. He also served as colonel of the First Regiment of the Ulster County Militia for twenty years.

Abraham (1711–?) first married Marritje Roosa and then Marritje Hasbrouck.

Lronardu (1714–?) married Rachel Hoogeyeling.

Jacob (1717–?) married Pieternella Bruyn.

ABRAHAM HASBROUCK (?–1717), along with his father, fled form Calais, France, to Mannheim, Germany, with other Huguenot families. Abraham also lived in Holland and England, where he served in the English army. His brother Jean married Anna Deyo, daughter of Christian Deyo, and in 1673, they came to Esopus with their unmarried children, Mary and Hester. In 1675, Abraham sailed to Boston and joined his brother at Esopus. Abraham married Maria Deyo (1653–1741), daughter of Christian Deyo, in 1676 at Hurley. Abraham served as a lieutenant in the Kingston and New Paltz foot companies in 1685 and rose to captain in 1686. He was a member of the assembly in 1698–99.

Children:

Rachel (1679–?) married Louis du Bois Jr., son of Louis du Bois and Catherine Blanchan, in 1701. They had three children.

Joseph (1684–?) married Elsie Schoonmaker, daughter of Jochem H. Schoonmaker and Petronella Slecht.
Solomon (1686–?) married Sarah van Wagenen, daughter of Jacob Aertsen van Wagenen and Sara Pels.
Daniel (1692–?) married Wyntje Deyo, daughter of Abraham Deyo and Elsie Clearwater.
Benjamin (1696–?) married Jannetje DeLange.

Gerrit Cornelissen Van Nieuwkirk (1631–1695) traveled to the New Netherlands with his second wife, Chieltje Cornelis Slecht, their infant son, Disje, and his twelve-year-old younger brother, Mattheus (1642–1705), on the ship *Moesman* in 1659. The baby died soon after they arrived. Gerrit first settled at Flatbush, Long Island, and then sold his land in 1665. About March 1669, he purchased eighty-five acres of land in Hurley. He enlisted in Captain Henry Pauling's foot company in 1670.

Children:
Cornelis Gerretse (1662–1696) married Jannetje Jansz Kunst (1664–after 1729), daughter of Jan Barrentsen Kunst and Jocomyntje Cornelis Slecht, in 1683. Jennetje's sister, Hellete Kunst, married Nicholas Roosevelt, and they are the ancestors of President Theodore Roosevelt. Cornelis served as a private under Captain Hendrickus Beekman in the Kingston Horse Company from 1686 to 1687. They had seven children. Their oldest son, Gerrit (1684–1724), married Grietjen Ten Eyck. They had seven children, and he is believed to have been the builder of the original Newkirk/Hofler House.
Arien Gerritsen (1663–?) married Lysbeth Lambertsen Brink (1666–?), daughter of Lambert Huyberts Brink, in 1686. They had eight children.
Jan (Johannes) Gerretse (1666–?) married Yiyjen Deckers in 1687.
Neetje Gerretse (1667–1706) first married Peter Crispell (1664–1695), son of Anthony Crispell and Maria Blanchan, in 1689. They had three children. She then married Johannes Schepmoes in 1697. They had one child.
Gerretje Gerretse (1668–1739) first married Jan Barentsen Kunst, son of Barent Kunst and brother of Jannetje Kunst. They had one child. She then married Jacob du Bois, son of Louis du Bois and Catherine Blanchan. They had eleven children.
Ginitje married Salomon du Bois, brother of Jacob.

PIETER PIETERSEN OSTRANDER (1657–?) arrived at New Amsterdam in 1661 with his mother, Geesje Jans, his sister, Tryntje Pieters, and his stepfather, Avent Teunissen, onboard the *De St. Han Baptiste* from Amsterdam. The family settled on Coney Island but soon moved to Wiltwyck in 1663. Pieter married Rebecca Taphagen (1662–?), daughter of Willem Jansen Taphagen and Joose Willems, in 1679. In 1699, Pieter briefly used the last name Noorstrand, but the following year, he used an early version of Ostrander. By 1716, he was using the name Pieter Ostrander Sr.; his son was using the name Pieter Ostrander Jr. Pieter and Rebecca had thirteen children.

Children:
Pieter (1680–?) married Rachel Dingman in 1704.
Willem (1682–?) married Marytje d'Hooges van Etten in 1705.
Arent (1684–?) married Geertny Maasen van Bloomindal in 1710. They had nine children.
Tryntje (1686–before 1700)
Johannes (1688–?) married Elizabeth Van den Burghin 1713.
Teunis (1691–?) married Maritje Suyland in 1718.
Hendrick (1693–?) married Elizabeth van Bommel in 1724.
Rachel (1698–?) married Doloman Terwilliger in 1720.
Geesje (1700–?) married Ary Roosa in 1722.
Rebecca (1702–?) married Johannes D'Hooges van Etten.
Jacob (1706–?) married Maritje Roosa (1706–?), daughter of Evert Aries Roosa and Tientje Van Etton, in 1726.[24]

CAPTAIN HENRY PAULING (?–1692) was born in England. He came to New York with the duke's expedition in 1664. He married Neeltje Roosa (1652–?), daughter of Aldert Heymans Roosa and Wyntie Arens, in 1676. He held many positions, including captain of the foot company, served on several commissions and helped disband the garrison under Sir Francis Lovelace. He was honorably discharged in 1670. In 1684, he was appointed high sheriff of Ulster County and served until 1689. He purchased land in Ulster County and seven hundred acres of land in Duchess County known as the Pawling purchase. He served as a farmer, one who regulated and collected excise taxes on brewers and distillers. Because of this position, his name is found in many court cases regarding claims for fines against brewers and distillers, such as Louis du Bois and Matthew Blanchan.

Children:

Jane married John Cock of Marbletown in 1706.

Weyntje (1679–?) married Richard Broadhead.

Jan/John (1681–?) first married Aagie de Witt, and they had eight children. His second wife was Ephira.

James (1683) died young.

Aldert (1682–?) married Catherine Beekman Rutsen in 1726. They had no children. He was an ensign in the Marbletown militia and a representative in the New York Assembly from 1726 to 1737. The town of Pawling, New York, is named after him.

Anne (1687–before 1739) married Tireck de Witt in 1708.

Henry (1689–1739) married Jacomyntie Kunst, daughter of Cornelius Barrenstein Kunst and Jacomyntie Slecht, in 1713. They had seven children. They moved to Pennsylvania in 1719. Their son, Colonel Levi, returned to Ulster County and served in politics, as well as the military. He married Helena Burhans in 1749.

Marie (1692–?) married Thomas van Keuren.

Captain Mattys Ten Eyck (1658–1741) was born in New Amsterdam. His parents, Coenradt Ten Eyck (1616–1687) and Maria Boele (1622–1682), and his siblings, Maria (1646–1694), Jacob (1647–1693) and Dirck (1648–1711), arrived there between 1648 and 1651. In Hurley, he married Jannetje Roosa (1656–1726), daughter of Aldert Roosa and Wyntke d'Joog, in 1679. They had eight children who survived infancy.

Children:

Aldert (1680–1710) married Maria van Vechten (1687). They lived in New Jersey.

Maria (1682–1760) married Tireck Matthysen Van Keuren (1682–1742), the son of Mattys Mattysen Van Keuren and Tjatje De Witt, in Kingston in 1702. They had thirteen children.

Wyntje (1684–?) married Jan Hendricksen about 1705.

Marguerite (1689–1743) first married Gerrit Herritse Newkirk (1684–1722), son of Cornelius Gerritse Newkirk and Jannetje Kunst, about 1710. They had six children. She then married William Burhans (1686), the son of Jan Burhans and Helena Taphagen, in 1731 They had one known child. William had a second marriage to Catherine Kool, widow of Jacob Van Etton, in 1749.

Andrias (1691–1769) married Ariaantje Crispell (1694–?), daughter of Pieter Crispell and Neeltje Gerritse Newkirk, in 1712.
Jacob (1694–1753) married either Neeltje Hardenburgh or Jemeyma van Ness (1700–1792).
Sara (1697–?) married Lawrence Courtright, son of Hendrick Jansen Kortreght and Catherine Hansen Webber, in 1715. They had six children.
Rachel (1699–1771) married Cornelis Newkirk, son of Cornelius Gerritse Newkirk and Jannetje Kunst, in 1720. They had six children.
Abraham (1699–1747) a twin to Rachel, married Janneken Elmendorf (?–after 1747), daughter of Conradt Elmendorf and Blandina Giersteeden, in 1726. They had two children.

Captain Mattys's sister Maria came to Ulster County and married Wessel Wesselsen Ten Brouck in 1670 in Hurley. His younger brother, Hendrick (1656–1721), born in New Amsterdam, married Petronella De Witt in 1675. His other siblings either stayed in New Amsterdam or lived in Albany.

Mattys was locally known as "Captain" due to his rank in the local militia. He participated in the French and Indian War. He was a farmer and smart businessman. In 1709, he and his son-in-law, Gerrit Newkirk, purchased land and built a grain mill. They shared in this operation until 1766, when he sold his share to Benjamin Newkirk.

From 1720 to 1722, he served as town assessor. From 1720 to 1722, he served as town trustee, and in 1723, he was appointed poor master for one year. In 1724, he served as tax collector and constable, and in 1725, he was town supervisor.

JACOB JANSEN VAN ETTON (1632–1693) was born in Etton, Holland. He immigrated to New Netherlands about 1658. He immediately settled at Wiltwyck. In *Olde Ulster*, the author describes a man known as "Jan the Brabanter." He owned a lot in the stockade, appears as a corporal during the Esopus Mutiny and was an in-law of Aert Pietersen Tach. Jacob Van Etton (meaning "from Etton," a village in North Brabant, Holland), was head farmer on the farm of Aert Pietersen Tach, which was destroyed by the Indians in the Second Esopus War. It is believed that the two Jacobs are the same person. Tach disappeared and was presumed killed in the attack, leaving behind a wife, Annetje. It was later discovered that Tach had deserted his wife before the attack and returned to Holland.

Tach's estate had many debts, including wages owed to Jacob Van Etton. Tach granted Annteje a divorce in August 1664 at Fort Amsterdam. In January 1665, she married "Jacob Jansen, young man of Etten, in Brabant."[25]

Jacob signed the petition for a minister in Esopus in 1676 and signed the Oath of Allegiance to England in 1689. He and his wife had ten children.

Children:

Jan (1666–?) married Jannetje Roosa (1670–?), daughter of Captain Arie Roosa and Marie Pels, in 1690. He then married Cornelia Van Aaken, widow of Jan Chamers, in 1731. He and his first wife had ten children. He was an elder in the Kingston Dutch Reformed Church.

Sytje (1668–?) married Jan Everts, sometimes listed as Terwillinger from Holland, in 1685. They had twelve children and lived in Marbletown.

Arien (1670–1702) married Catherine Crom of Wawarsing in 1694. They had five children, and after Arien's death, Catherine married Hendrick Cortreght in 1703.

Pieter (1675–after 1730) married Eva d'Hooges, daughter of Anthony d'Hooges and Eva Bratt, in 1697. They had seven children, lived in Hurley and then, in 1720, settled in Duchess County.

Petronella (1675–after 1736) married Aldert Roosa, son of Captain Arie Heymans Roosa (1645–1725) and Marie Pels (1654–1714), in 1696. No children are recorded.

Heiltje (1679–?) married William Van Vredenburg of Kinderhook in 1699. They had thirteen children and lived in Kingston.

Emanuel (1681–?) married Antje d'Hooges, daughter of Anthony d'Hooges and Eva Bratt, in 1702. They had seven children and lived in Marbletown. Sometime after 1714, they moved to New Jersey.

Tietje (1684–?) married Evert Roosa (1697–1749), son of Arie Alderts Roosa and Weynte Aend Ariinz d'Jong, in 1702. They had ten children.

Jacobus (1686–1759) married Rebecca Roosa (1689–1767), daughter of Jan Alderts Roosa and Hilligond Willensen Van Buren, in 1710. They had ten children. They moved to Duchess County about 1720.

Geesjen (1688–?) married Jacob Decker Jr. of Marbletown in 1704. They had five children.

Major Jacob Aertsen Van Wagenen (1652–1716), son of Aert Jacobsen Van Wagenen and Annetje Gerrets, married Sara Everts Pels (1659–?), daughter of Evert Pels and Jannetje Symens, in 1677. There are many references to his father in the early records of Wiltwyck, including his purchase of ninety-seven acres in 1660, bordering the properties of Tjerck Claesen de Witt, Aert Pietersen Tach and Jans Schoon. In 1679, Jacob was chosen as deacon of the Dutch Church of Kingston. He and Sara had fifteen children.

Children:

Annatje (1678–?) married Jan Heermans (1677–?), son of Jan Heermans and Engelte Breetede. They had three children.

Aert Aertsen (1679–1740) married Marytje Louw (1686–1733), daughter of Pieter Cornelisse Louw and Lysbeth Blanchan, in 1705. They had ten children. He probably built the stone house identified as the home of Peter Van Wagenen.

Evert Aertsen (1681–?) married Hillegond Vanhet\ymingen (1668–?), daughter of Claes Jansen Vanheymingen and Janneken Kiersen, in 1701. They had six children. In 1712, they moved to Poughkeepsie.

Gerrit Aartz (1682–1709) was killed by a tree limb cut down by his father.

Rebecca Aartz (1685–?) married Jan Freer (1682–?), son of Hugo Freer and Jannetje Wibdu, in 1706. They had eight children.

Geertje Aartzen (1686–?) married Jacob Gerritse Decker (1684–?), son of Gerrit Jans Decker and Magdalena Schut, in 1709. They had twelve children.

Jannetje Aertsen (1689–?) married Johannis Turk (1687–1736), son of Jacobus Turk and Catryntje Vanbenthuysen, in 1711. They had eight children.

Gerrit Aertsen (1691–?)

Symon Jacobse (1692–1755?) married Sara du Bois (1699–1759), daughter of Solomon du Bois and Tryntje Gerrits, in 1720. They had eight children.

Jacob Aerse (1695–1720?)

Benjamin Aartsen (1696–?), married Elizabeth Vandenburg, daughter of Gysbert Vandenberg and Dievertje Masten, in 1726. They had seven children.

Abraham Aartse (1697–1787) married Hillegond Crispell (1704–1774), daughter of John Crispell and Grietje Janse Rosa, in 1726. They had ten children, the middle five died in infancy. His house is in Wagendale. He signed the Articles of Association of Hurley. In 1797, he donated the land where the first church on Maple Hill was built. It burned in 1846, and his son Abram, along with George LeFever, built a new church on the site of the present-day Bloomington Reformed Dutch Church.

Sarah Jacobse Aartsen (1701–?) married Solomon Hasbrouck (1686–1753), son of Abraham Hasbrouck and Maria Deyo, in 1721. They had five children.

Issac Aartsen (1703–1794?) married Catrina Freer (1703–?) in 1723.

In 1688, '89 and '93, Jacob was a trustee of the Corporation of Kingston. In 1682, he purchased six hundred acres of land—the area of Nieuw Dorp, now the town of Esopus—from Colonel Henry Beekman, who purchased it from the Esopus Indians that same year. This area is referred to as Magowasinginck Patent, meaning "at the place of the large stone," referring to the large rocks in the Rondout Creek near what would become Wagendale and, later, Creek Locks.[26]

Here he built a long, low, stone house. The initials "JA" and the year "1699" are carved into a foundation stone. It can be surmised that the house was probably built before this to accommodate his large family. The 1699 appears to mark the large addition in the back. The house is located near the bank of the Rondout Creek, near the present village of Crook Locks, formerly called Wagendale. A fire destroyed the building in 1929. The house, minus the addition, was rebuilt over the remaining stone.

Around the house are three other stone houses all built by Van Wagenen. An old burial ground for the early settlers is located on a hill nearby. Across the creek lies another Van Wagenen stone house, built in 1745 by Joseph. His brother Isaac later became the owner of the slave Sojourner Truth, and he encouraged her to force the court in Kingston to recover her son, Peter, who had been sold into slavery and unlawfully taken out of the state. Her son was eventually returned, and Isaac set Sojourner free.[27]

In 1703, a law was enacted to create a road from New Jersey to Albany. Its path lay directly through Ulster County. Jacob Aertsen was one of three commissioners appointed to lay out the roads in this county.[28]

Jacob's house passed to his wife, Sara, and then to his grandson, Jacob Aerts (1707–1775), oldest son of Aert Aertsen and Marytje Low. Jacob Aerts married Sara Freer (1708–1778), his first cousin, daughter of Jan Freer and Rebecca Van Wagenen. The house remained in the Van Wagenen family until the late 1800s.

Cornelis Wynkoop (?–1676) and his wife, Maria Janse Langedyck (?–1679), moved to Esopus from Rensselaerwyck between 1664 and 1667. On May 30, 1662, he made a lease of lots one and sixteen at Esopus to Lambert Huybertse. In April 1669, he was appointed commissart of Kingston and held the position until 1674. In 1673, he became the *scheppen* of Hurley. He became an elder of the Kingston Dutch Reformed Church in 1671.

Children:

Major Johannis (?–between 1730 and 1733) first married Judith Fransen Bloodgood (1665–?), daughter of Captain Frans Jansen Bloetgood and Lysbeth Jans, in 1687. They had three children. Their son, Cornelis, married Hendricka Newkirk, daughter of Adtian Gerritsen Newkirk and Lysbeth Lambertsen. He then married Cornelia Ten Broeck (?–1729), daughter of Major Dirk Wesselse Ten Broeck and Christina Cornelise Van Buren, in 1696. They had five children. Johannis served as a trustee, magistrate and assessor of Kingston.

Maria (dates unknown) married Moses du Puis, son of Nicholas du Puis, about 1680. They had eleven children.

Evert (1665–1746) first married Gertrude Elmendorf, daughter of Jacobus and Geertje Aertse Elmendorf, in 1688. He then married Antje Kiersted, daughter of Roelof Kiersted and Eyke Roosa, before 1707. They had nine children. He served as a magistrate and trustee of Kingston.

Benjamin (1675–after 1737) married Femmetje van der Heul (1671–after 1737), daughter of Abraham and Trintje Hendericks van der Heulm, in 1697. He was a goldsmith. His slave, London, a Spanish Indian, was indicted, along with others, for plotting to burn New York City in 1741. Benjamin and Femmetje had seven children.

Chapter Two

HURLEY IS REBUILT AND GROWS

The Great Hardenburgh Patent

In 1704, Cornelius Cool, Ariaen Gerritsen, Mattys Ten Eyck, Jacob du Bois, Johannis Schepmoes, Roelof Swartwout, Cornelis Lemmerse, Pieter Pieterse, Louren Osterhaut and Jannetje Newkirk petitioned Governor Lord Edward Hyde Cornbury, an agent for Queen Anne, for a tract of land. The land lay west of Kingston and Hurley. Cool and his partners wanted the land for grazing cattle and for its vast supply of wood. Cornbury granted the request and, at Cool's expense, commissioned a survey. The surveyor took his time, and over a year and a half passed before it was completed. During this time, Major Johannes Hardenburgh and his partners—Leonard Lewis, Phillip Rockley, William Nottingham, Benjamin Faneuil, Peter Fauconier and Robert Luritng—slipped in a similar petition for the same tract of land. With some backdoor wrangling, Cornbury granted Hardenburgh's petition. Hardenburgh then negotiated with the Indians for the sale of this land, although as he and his partners worked, the size of the tract increased until the final total reached over a million and a half acres. The land encompassed parts of present-day Ulster, Greene, Orange, Delaware and Sullivan Counties.

Cool and his partners did not rest on their laurels. They filed several complaints regarding the impropriety of the grant going to Hardenburgh. Some felt that the Cool petition had not been written or filed properly;

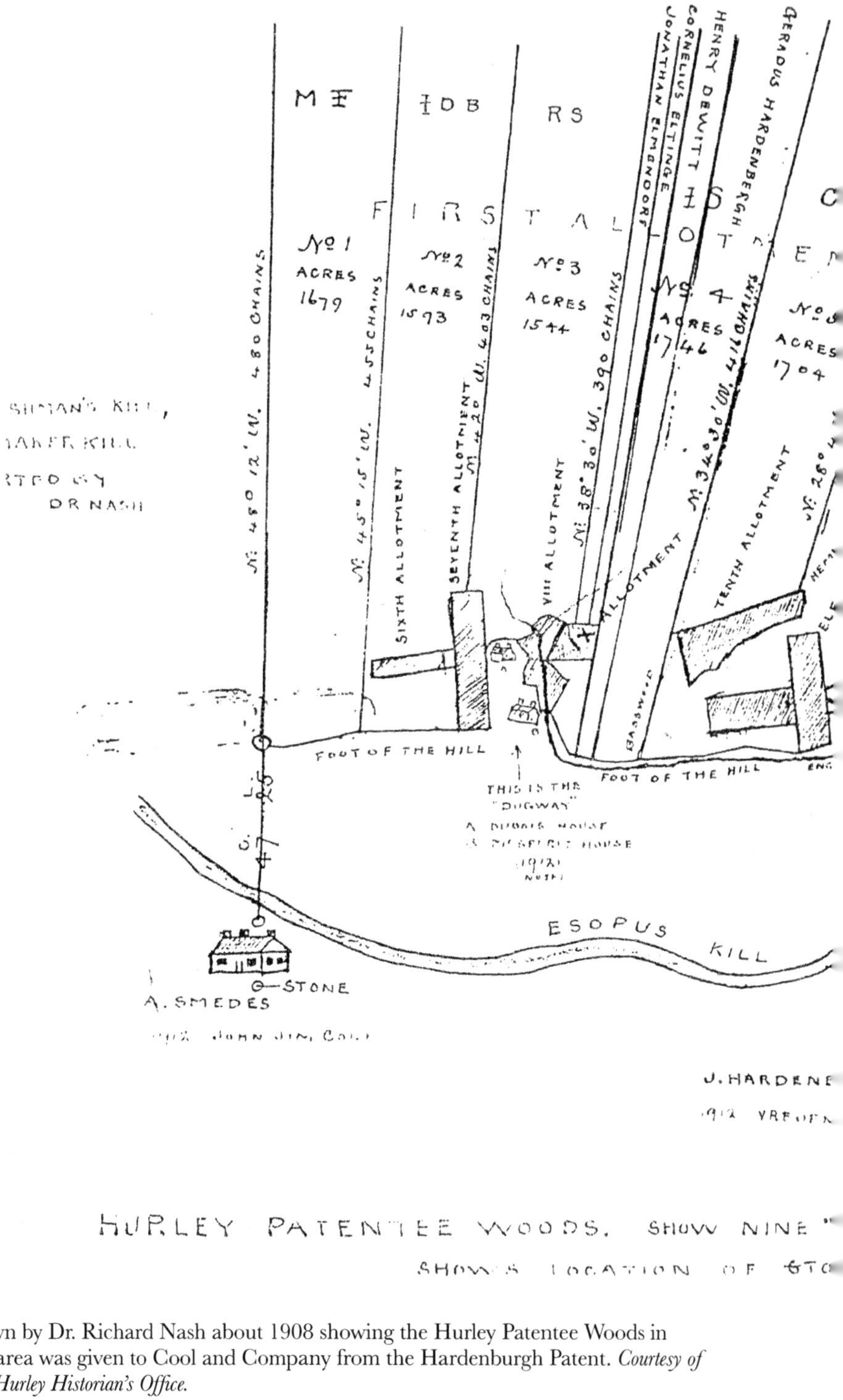

A map drawn by Dr. Richard Nash about 1908 showing the Hurley Patentee Woods in 1708. This area was given to Cool and Company from the Hardenburgh Patent. *Courtesy of the Town of Hurley Historian's Office.*

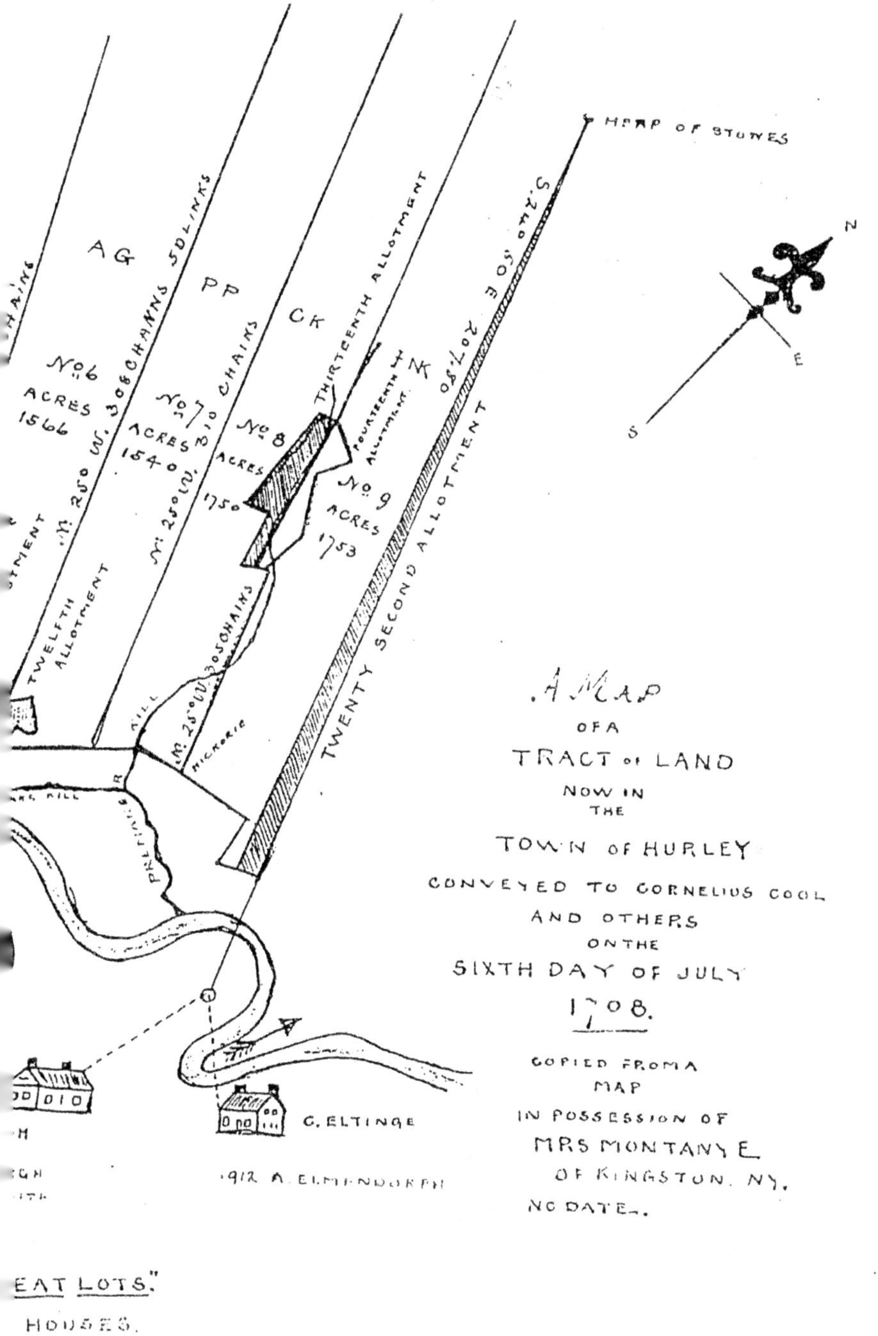
HEAP OF STONES
N
E
S
AG
PP
CK
NK
No. 6
ACRES
1566
No. 7
ACRES
1540
No. 8
ACRES
1750
No. 9
ACRES
1753
THIRTEENTH ALLOTMENT
FOURTEENTH ALLOTMENT
TWELFTH ALLOTMENT
TWENTY SECOND ALLOTMENT
N. 25° W. 308 CHAINS 50 LINKS
N. 25° W. 310 CHAINS
N. 25° W. 305 CHAINS
HICKORIC
C. ELTINGE
1912 A. ELMENDORPH
"EAT LOTS."
HOUSES.
A MAP
OF A
TRACT OF LAND
NOW IN
THE
TOWN OF HURLEY
CONVEYED TO CORNELIUS COOL
AND OTHERS
ON THE
SIXTH DAY OF JULY
1708.
COPIED FROM A
MAP
IN POSSESSION OF
MRS MONTANYE
OF KINGSTON. NY.
NO DATE.

others felt that Lord Cornbury actually benefitted from the transaction. In the end, all of the protesting fell on somewhat deaf ears, and on April 20, 1708, the matter was settled. Lord Cornbury awarded the property to Hardenburgh and Company, with the stipulation that Hardenburgh's group sell a small tract to Cool and his partners. Cornbury granted a small pasture to the residents of Hurley as a common land. In July 1708, the partners conveyed their interest to Cornelius Cool, Ariaen Gerritsen, Mattys Ten Eyck, Jacob du Bois, Johannis Schepmoes, Roelof Swartwout, Cornelis Lemmerse, Pieter Pieterse, Louren Osterhaut and Jannetje Newkirk in joint tenancy.

HURLEY HOUSES

Benjamin Newkirk/Hofler House
Hurley Mountain Road

In 1709, the holders of the Hurley Patentee Woods sold this property with the Premaeker Kill to Captain Mattys Ten Eyck and his son-in-law, Garret Nieuwkirk, with the privilege of building one or more mills and dams as they saw fit. On August 19, 1712, Captain Ten Eyck gave his half to Newkirk.

MAJOR ADRIAN WYNKOOP (1726–1795) and **COLONEL CORNELIUS D. WYNKOOP** (1732–1796) were the sons of Cornelis and grandsons of Major Johannes Wynkoop.

Cornelis married Maria C. Ruehl, daughter of Gustav Martin and Maria Margaretha Roel, in 1760. He served as captain of the First Company, Southeast District of Marbletown, in the Third Regiment of Ulster County under Colonel Levi Pawling, Lieutenant Colonel Jacob Hoenbeck, Major Johannis Cantine and Major Joseph Hasbroeck. The couple had nine children.

Major Adrian married Catherine Louw (1733–1796) in 1754. In 1775, he was a member of the committee in Hurley to select delegates to attend the New York provincial convention. He was major of the First Regiment of Ulster County. He led the artillery unit that defended Kingston and delayed the British advance into Hurley, saving valuable wheat crops. He and his wife had no children.

Major Cornelius D. Wynkoop (1734–1792) first married Leah du Bois (1742–?), daughter of Cornelis du Bois and Margaret Houghtaling, in 1762. They had two children. He then married Anna Gansevoort (1744–1794), daughter of Harmen and Margaret Gansevoort, in 1778. They had three children. He was major of the Third Regiment and was appointed lieutenant colonel in 1775 and colonel in 1776.

The murder of Colonel Cornelius D. Wynkoop shocked the village. The story was documented in the *Catskill Packet* on December 10, 1792:

> *Murder in Ulster County*
>
> *The following horrid transaction occurred last Thursday week at Hurley, a few miles below Esopus. Col. Cornelius D. Wynkoop of that place, hearing a disturbance in his kitchen, amongst his Negroes, requested his son to know the cause and put a stop to it, his son accordingly went and made use of some harsh treatment to the one he thought most at fault, who immediately ran out of the house, took up an axe and bid defiance to anyone that would dare approach him. The Col. then went to the door himself to reprimand him for his villainous conduct, when the Negro went at him with the axe and sunk it in his head in such a shocking manner as to put an immediate period to his existence. The Negro then made off, but soon after returned and asked a fellow servant if his master was dead; being answered in the affirmative, he again ran off, and we do not learn of his having been since heard of.*

The *Packet*, a fortnight later, announced the arrest and jailing of the murderer. The tale is told that the slave was found by following the tracks in the snow of other slaves, who were taking him food. These tracks led to his hideout under the porch.[29]

Crispell Parsonage
Main Street

Johannes Crispell acquired the property in 1725. The house was built on the foundation of a smaller house, probably built by Johannes shortly after he purchased the property. Johannes married Ann Margaret Roosa,

A view of the Crispell Cottage and Dr. Richard Ten Eyck House coming up from Wynkoop Road, circa 1900. The church is to the left. *Courtesy of the Town of Hurley Historian's Office.*

and they had three children. He was the stepson of Johannes Schepmoes. Johannes Crispell also built a barn to store his horse, cattle and grain. In 1764, their son Petrus inherited the house. During the Revolution, Petrus served as a private in the First Ulster Militia foot company under Colonel Johannes Snyder. The original building contained two rooms and a hall. Petrus's son John and John's wife, Jane Hasbrouck, added the kitchen after 1798. John's two sons departed from their family's farming tradition and became prominent doctors in the area. Having no heirs to take over the farm, an aging John sold the house lot to the trustees of the Hurley Reformed Church in November 1839 for $1,600. At that point, the property contained the house, a large barn and several outbuildings. At least two outbuildings sat to the right of the house near present-day Route 209. There was also a well in the backyard with a rope and bucket.

After 1851, the outbuildings were removed to create a parking area for the parishioners' carriages. Two sheds were constructed to shelter the horses. In April 1882, a severe storm blew through; lightning struck the chimney of the house and then forked in three different directions. It damaged the building and also zapped the telephone in the nearby Ontario & Western Railroad depot. The house still serves as the parsonage today.

Dr. Richard Ten Eyck House
Main Street

This lot, across from the church and parsonage, dates back to about 1663, when the village was expanded. The current house sits on the site of an earlier, smaller cottage. Dr. Richard Ten Eyck inherited the property from his father, Matthew, who bought the property in 1772 from land originally owned by Aldert Heymans Roosa. The property had remained in the Roosa family until 1772. It was bounded by Main Street, Marbletown Road (Old Route 209), the mill brook and his father's pastureland, now Depot Street. Richard built the house as a wedding gift for his wife, Janet Baker. Dr. Ten Eyck was obviously wealthy, and in addition to being a doctor, he also owned a mill, brewery and distillery on the property. He grew bread grains, had extensive orchards and raised sheep. The house is two stories, with a center hall with a stone lean-to that served as a kitchen. The fireplaces are centered on the end wall in each room. The center hall contains the stairway, with a single room on each side, and the first and second floors are identical. The house was

The front side of the Ten Eyck house, circa 1900. *Courtesy of the Hurley Museum.*

built in the five-bay Georgian style popular from 1740 to 1820. In 1810, Dr. Ten Eyck owned fourteen slaves, who were mostly laborers. By 1830, the house was shared by the doctor, his oldest son, James, and James's family. The house remained in the family for over one hundred years, until it was sold to the Markle family. The Ten Eyck family is buried at the old cemetery.

Richter House (Houghtaling)
Old Route 209

The earliest traceable property owner is Charles Wylei, a miller. He owned a long stretch of property, of which this is a portion. He sold a section of the property to Willem Van Hardenburgh on April 12, 1712, for three pounds. On December 21, 1720, Willem sold this lot to Gerrit Konstapol, a weaver, along with a stone house, for forty-eight pounds, fifteen shillings. Tax records

The Richter House, circa 2001. Once owned by the Houghtalings', it lies on the east side of Old Route 209. *Courtesy of David Baker.*

show that the house was built by 1715. It is thought that Gerrit built a room onto the cottage to use as his commercial weaver's room. Gerrit married Margrietjen van Vliet in 1721. A 1743 deed for an adjoining property shows that Gerrit still owned the property at that time.

The Old Hotel
Main Street

This building, located near the corner of Main Street and Schoolhouse Lane, has gone by many names—Wynkoop Inn, the Van Sickle Inn and Tavern, the Continental Hotel and the Hurley Hotel. Built in 1716, it is believed to have been the oldest tavern in Ulster County. The Wynkoop Inn was the stop for the stage to Ellenville and Newark, New Jersey.

After the British burned Kingston in October 1777, this inn became the headquarters for General Clinton and the Committee of Safety. Early courts

The Wynkoop Inn on Main Street, circa 1890. This is probably what it looked like during the Revolution. *Courtesy of the Hurley Museum.*

The Van Sickle Inn and Tavern in the early 1900s after additions, including a store to the left. *Courtesy of George K. Van Sickle.*

Another view of the building, now the Centennial House, as shown on the sign. *Courtesy of George K. Van Sickle.*

were also held here. In 1880, Lewis Van Sickle owned it as the Hurley Hotel. By the early 1900s, the Van Sickle Inn and Tavern had become the first building in town to have electricity.

On March 18, 1909, the town awoke to smoke and flames. According to an eyewitness account by James M. Schmidt, Charley Du Mond had a grocery store in a small cottage across Schoolhouse Lane in front of the John P. Elmendorf house. Schmidt remembers seeing the minister, Reverend Vyverbers, sitting on the roof of the cottage pouring buckets of water down the exposed side to keeping it from igniting.[30]

In 1947, Lyman T. Schoonmaker, prominent builder and contractor, purchased the property now containing the Van Sickle store. Originally, it housed an electrical supply and hardware store, with two apartments above. It later became Schoonmaker's Gift Shop. A house built next door became the home of Bennie Krom. Eventually, the Krom house was remodeled and became the Hurley branch of the Kerhonkson National Bank. It is now Key Bank. The gift shop is now the parking lot.[31]

The original property extended down the lane to Mill Brook. On this property, Major Adrian Wynkoop and his wife lived in a wooden house. Adrian willed the property to his wife and his nephew, John C. Wynkoop. John purchased Catherine's share but predeceased her in 1796 and left his estate to his wife, Lydia.

Ten Eyck Store
Main Street

In a 1736 deed for the Van Deusen property next door, it states that this property belonged to Huybert Suylandt. He married Sara Crispell, daughter of Anthony Crispell and Maria Blanchan. In 1840, a store was established by Daniel P. Fuller. The store was also run by Abram Burger and a Mr. Drew. In 1851, Postmaster Frederick J. Schoonmaker rented space in the store for the post office. Subsequent postmasters—Dumont Elmendorf (1853), Abraham B. Houghtaling (1855) and Peter Crispell Jr. (1861)—did the same. Samuel Ten Eyck purchased the store, and in 1869, he was appointed postmaster. The post office remained until 1893, when Charles Du Mond took over the position of postmaster and moved it to his store.

The Ten Eyck Store on Main Street, circa 2001. It is located next to the Van Deusen House. *Courtesy of David Baker.*

About 1930, Josephine Ten Eyck ran an antique store in the front. She sold the property in 1956. In 1972, Michael and Claudia Stapleton purchased it and ran a drugstore there until 1978.

Du Mond/Spy/Guard House
Main Street

Jacob J. Van Etton and his wife, Annetje, are the first property owners on record. They are listed as residents in 1685, and the house, believed to be the oldest on Main Street, can be dated to about this time. The house later passed to their son, Jan. The house began as a stone two-room cottage with a stone dividing wall that originally supported a jambless fireplace in each room. The stone kitchen was added in the 1800s. In October 1777, the basement was used as a military prison, giving it the name "Guard

The Du Mond/Spy House, circa 1900. *Courtesy of the Hurley Museum.*

House." This is where the prisoner/spy Lieutenant Daniel Taylor was held, thus the other nickname, the "Spy House." The house is believed to be located on lot number three of the original 1662 village lots.

It remained in the family until 1933, when Clara Du Mond Sharaiff sold it to George C. Kent. The stone addition for a store was added in 1942. Another stone addition was added in back in the 1940s. A large barn once stood where the current driveway now sits.

The house served as the post office for a dozen years and as Kent's General Store in the 1940s.

The Spy and the Apple Tree

In October 1777, a Tory soldier was ordered to deliver a note from British general Sir Henry Clinton to General John Burgoyne in Saratoga. While traveling through Ulster County, near New Windsor, the courier, First Lieutenant Daniel Taylor of Captain Stewart's Company of the Ninth Regiment of the Royal Army, stumbled upon a picket guard of Colonel

Webb's regiment under the command of Lieutenant Howe. Many of the soldiers were dressed in stolen British uniforms. Taylor approached the soldiers and asked if they served under General Clinton. They replied affirmatively, and after he requested an audience, they took him to their general, Governor General George Clinton. Taylor soon discovered his mistake. He immediately swallowed the small silver ball containing the note, but Clinton saw it. In a letter to the Committee of Safety, Clinton wrote:

> *The letter from Clinton to Burgoyne, taken from Daniel Taylor, was enclosed in a small silver ball of an oval form, about the size of a fissee bullet, and shut with a screw in the middle. When he was taken and brought before me he swallowed it. I mistrusted this to be the case, from information I received, and administered to him a very strong emetic calculated to act either way. This had the desired effect; it brought it from him; but though close watched, he had the art to conceal it the second time.*
>
> *I made him believe I had taken one Captain Campbell, another messenger who was out on the same business; that I learned from him all I wanted to know, and demanded the ball on pain of being hung up instantly and cut open to search for it. This brought it forth.*[32]

The Americans took Taylor prisoner and subsequently court-martialed and sentenced him to death for treason. The message Taylor carried read as follows:

> *Fort Montgomery, October 8th, 1777*
> *Nous y voici, and nothing now between us but Gates. I sincerely hope little success of ours may facilitate your operations. In answer to your letter of the 28th Sept., by C.C.* [Captain Campbell] *I shall only say, I cannot presume to order, or even advise, for reasons obvious. I heartily wish you success.*
> *Faithfully yours,*
> *Gen Burgoyne H. Clinton*[33]

Much commentary has been made regarding this note; some even say that it was harmless and Taylor was not really a spy. This was wartime, and one would think that generals would not send notes simply to say hello. There was an answer to a previous letter, of which we do not know the contents. An operation was in motion to try to take New York State.

Taylor traveled north with Clinton's army until they reached Hurley, too late to aid the militia forces fighting to defend Kingston from the British attack. Clinton established a military outpost at Hurley, and the inns were filled with his officers. The Du Mond House became the Guard House and held all of the prisoners locked in the basement, including the spy. On October 18, the soldiers led Taylor down present-day Schoolhouse Lane to an apple tree behind the Wynkoop Inn.

The Honorable Charles G. De Witt, while editor of the *Ulster Sentinel*, took pains to interview persons who had had any connection with the Revolutionary events in this county and were still living. In the issue of that paper for September 26, 1827, he printed an account of the execution of Taylor, from which the following passage is quoted:

> *He had a long, thin rope around his neck, which was coiled and carried after him by a soldier. At Hurley, three miles from the smoking ruins of Kingston, Taylor was hung on the bough of an apple tree in a by street, not far from the village. The contrivance for his exit into eternity exemplified the rude expedition of the times. A hogshead was placed under the bough, the culprit mounted upon it, and the rope being fastened about it, and the rope being fastened above, the executioner kicked the hogshead over. He fainted, however, before the fatal kick was given, and thus had an apparently easy death. Jack Ketch, on this occasion, was performed by a soldier, who received, as per agreement, the dead man's boots for his reward.*

It is stated that Taylor's body was buried under the flagstone of the Van Sickle House. The body was moved to an unknown location; some say his family claimed the body, but no one really knows.

Brink/Fortiner House
Zandhoek Road

Located on the inside corner of the now one-way Zandhoek Road, this house sits next to the old Zandhoek School property. Named after John Fortiner, it was owned by Egbert Brink from 1720 to 1741. It passed to Brink's heirs about 1780, to Petrus Brink in 1792 and then to John E. McPherson. John Fortiner purchased it from McPherson in 1877.

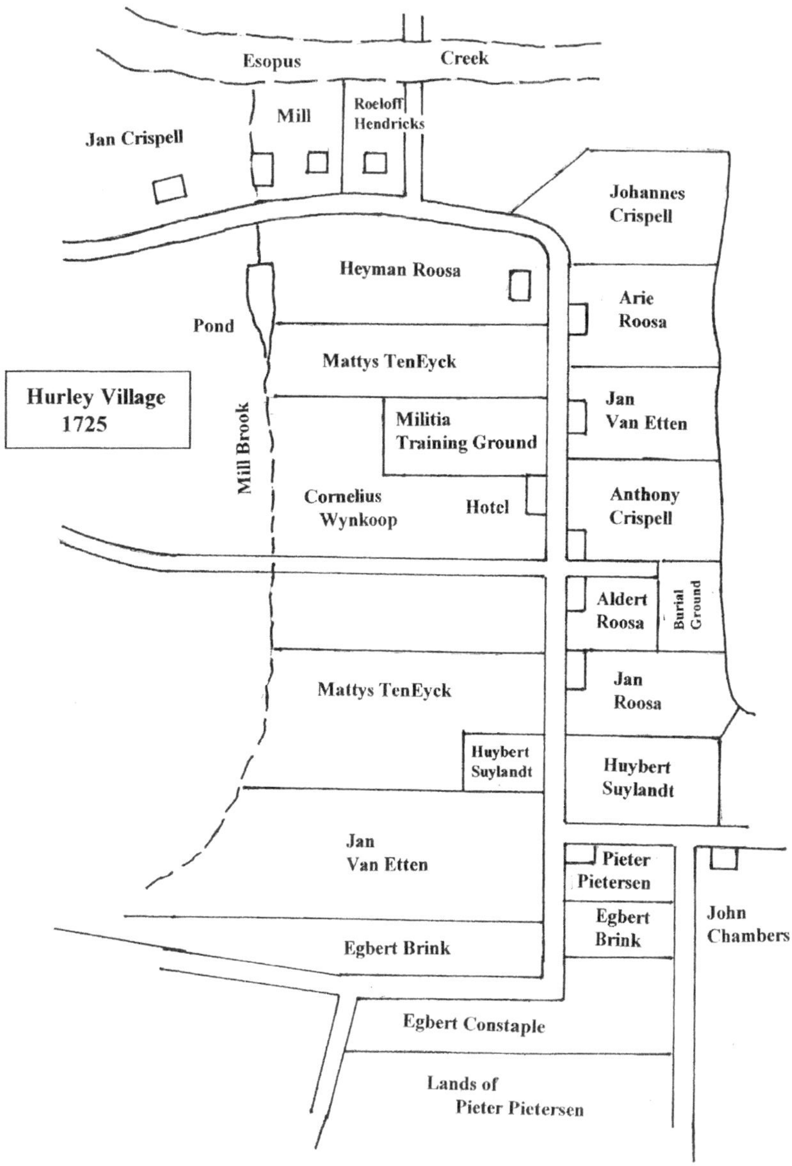

An illustrative map of Hurley's Main Street in 1725, put together using deeds and other documents. *Courtesy of David Baker.*

Polly Crispell Cottage
Main Street

Anthony Crispell, son of Pieter Crispell and Neltje Gerritsen Newkirk, built the house between 1720 and 1725 as a home with a workroom. He was a cordwainer, a worker who specializes in split leather and pigskin. His father died when he was four years old, and he was raised by his stepfather, Johannes Schepmoes, son of businessman and farmer Dirck Schepmoes. In 1719, Anthony married Lea Roosa, daughter of Hetman Roosa. He and Lea purchased two garden lots from her parents on Main Street. Soon after, he built the house and the leather shop.

The house was a one-room cottage with an English fireplace at the center of the east-end wall. The leather shop was in the west side of the house, heated by another fireplace on the back wall. He and his family lived in the house, and Lea was still living there in 1790.

The house passed out of the family until 1879, when Solomon Crispell and his wife, Sarah, purchased the home. She sold the property in 1884. No Polly ever lived in the house. One explanation for the name is that Sarah would sometimes be called "Sally," and when this was written in fancy script, it was mistaken for Polly. There are Polly Crispells listed in the census for that period, but it is not known if they ever lived in Hurley.

The Polly Crispell Cottage on Main Street, circa 1900. *Courtesy of the Hurley Museum.*

De Witt/Griffin House
Hurley Avenue

This property, which sits next door to the Schepmoes House, was a tenant farm under Christopher Newkirk that extended from Hurley Avenue to Lucas Avenue. There was a second tenant house on the property just northeast of the Griffin House on Hurley Avenue. It appears that the original tenant house was torn down, and a Victorian was built over part of the foundation.

Christopher De Witt either inherited or bought the property from his uncle, Christopher Newkirk. Christopher N. De Witt was born and raised in the Newkirk/Hofler House. His parents also lived there. Christopher married Anna while running the Newkirk farm and later moved to the Hurley Avenue house. He served as Ulster County supervisor and on the New York State legislature as a Republican. He also served as town supervisor from 1896 to 1900.

William J. Griffin, a financier for the reservoir as well as a lawyer, purchased the house from De Witt in 1924 and changed it to its present form.

The De Witt/Griffin House on Hurley Avenue, circa 2009. *Author's collection.*

Colonel John P. Elmendorf House/Hurley Heritage Museum
Main Street

In 1689, Johannis d'Hooges owned the property, which may have contained a house. The property was included in the estate of his widow, Grietje (Margarietje) d'Hooges. It is believed that the original house was a side-by-side duplex. The house was owned by Coenrad Elmendorf (1710–1789). He married Sara du Bois in 1734. He is listed as purchasing land just after his marriage. His son, Petrus (1748–?) later inherited the house. Petrus is noted as the homeowner in the 1798 tax rolls. He is also noted as the tavern keeper for the Half Moon Tavern across the street. Petrus married Annetje Du Mond (1748–1823) in 1776. They had five children, including their son, Petrus, also known as Petrus Jr. and Peter P. Petrus Jr. (1785–?), who married Janneke (Jane) in 1808. They had a son named John P.

John (?–1856) served as town clerk from 1816 to 1822. He also fought in the War of 1812 and was the town school inspector from 1813 to 1844.

The Jonathan P. Elmendorf House and Hurley Heritage Museum, circa 1900. *Courtesy of the Hurley Museum.*

MacKinnen/Captain Newkirk House
Dug Hill Road and Hurley Mountain Road

The first building on this property was in the style of rural Hudson Valley Dutch, built about 1700. It was originally one story and a half with a full basement and a Dutch jambless fireplace. The upper story was used to store grain. The smoke from the fireplace would keep out rodents and insects.

The second building was a free-standing, rural, Georgian-style cottage built about 1740. There are jambless English-style fireplaces on each end. The two buildings form a duplex with no doors connecting the two. A stone kitchen room was added to the newer building before the Revolution. The main section of the house was added recently.

This lot was part of the Hurley Patentee Woods. It was the home of Captain Cornelius C. Newkirk (1752–1832). He married Sarah Kiersted. He was a sergeant for the Kingston Horse Company and the First Ulster Light Brigade and became a first lieutenant in 1778 and a captain in 1779. His daughter Catherine married Ten Eyck De Witt. He deeded his property, lot number three of the patentee to his son Christopher (1782–

The Captain Newkirk House on the corner of Dug Hill Road and Hurley Mountain Road. *Courtesy of the Town of Hurley Historian's Office.*

1876) in his will, probated in 1832. Christopher married Cornelia W. Ten Eyck (1790–1859).

There is a survey dated April 5, 1686, of a tract of eighty-five acres of land on the north side of Esopus Kill in Hurley, called Old Bowery, laid out for Gerrit Cornelius by Phillip Wells, surveyor.[34]

New Dorp
Main Street

This land borders the property of the stone schoolhouse. It was owned by A.S. Houghtaling from 1875 to 1880. In 1900, it was owned by Calvin Berhams, who ran a blacksmith shop. When he retired, the shop was taken over by Grant Smith. Behind the shop was a wagon maker's shop belonging to Charles Markle. In the 1900s, it was a tearoom.

Hardenburgh House
Schoolhouse Lane

At a meeting of the trustees of the town of Hurley on December 24, 1728, the trustees granted Major Johannis Hardenburgh nine acres of land along the King's Highway (Old Route 209). In the following January, Hardenburgh purchased the property containing the house and mill. This property was common land.

In 1743, Hardenburgh and his wife, Catherine, signed a rental agreement with Abraham DeLameter for the house and lot containing ten acres of woods and pasture, along with a ground mill, milldam, brew house and brewery. In April 1743, Gerardus Hardenburgh purchased land between the house lot and mill property.

For a long time, this house was believed to have been the birthplace and childhood home of Isabelle Hardenburgh, otherwise known as Sojourner Truth. It has since been determined that she actually was born in a Hardenburgh house in present-day Rosendale, which used to be a part of the town of Hurley.

The Hardenburgh House at the end of Schoolhouse Lane, circa 1900. A Dutch barn once stood here. *Courtesy of the Town of Hurley Historian's Office.*

The Stone Schoolhouse
Main Street

This property was once part of a single tract of land owned by Mattys Ten Eyck and then his son, Matthew. This land extended to today's Schoolhouse Lane. The school was constructed with locally quarried limestone; it was one story and measured twenty-five feet long by twenty feet wide. A large fireplace was built on the west side of the room. Black children sat at the back of the room.

In 1836, the community felt it necessary to modernize. They tore down the schoolhouse and used the stone to build the new one at the end of Main Street on the Zandhoek one-way.

The earliest record (1912) yet discovered might be seen in "Ulster County Wills," compiled by Anjou. It is the will of James Scott, merchant of Hurley, dated December 21, 1754:

> *Residue of the estate, after payment of debts, to be converted into money, put at interest, taking good security, and the executor, Levi Pauling, to pay annually towards the support of an English schoolmaster for the Town of Hurley, and as far westerly as Levi Pauling's, Esq., interest on the same. Witnessed by Isaac Roosa, Petrus Roosa, Egbert Roosa. Proved March 20, 1755.*[35]

It was at this schoolhouse where it is said that schoolboys saluted George Washington as he came through town in 1782 after receiving

> *an address of welcome at the hotel below by the president of the village. This little salute so pleased the famous man that he invited the boys to the neighboring tavern and there, patting them on the head, allowed them, according to the custom of the day, to take a sip of wine from his own glass.*
>
> *Old John Ostrander (born 1744), still remembered by many people in the village and whose house was situated near the present brick house of the Ostrander family, was one of those school boys and delighted to tell the story of his meeting the "Father of this Country."*[36]

If this account is to be believed, and if his birth year is correct, John would have been thirty-eight at the time.

Colonel Charles De Witt (1727–1787) served as a colonel for the Second Ulster County Militia Regiment. He was the son of Johannes de Witt and Mary Brodhead and grandson of Andries de Witt. In 1754, he married Blandina du Bois (1731–1765). He enjoyed an illustrious political career beginning in 1768, representing Ulster County in New York's Colonial Assembly, where he served until his death. In 1775, the Assembly was replaced by the Provincial Congress, where he continued to serve as a member of the committees approving the Continental Congress and the Declaration of Independence and drafting New York's first state constitution. He served on the Committee of Safety in 1777. In 1784, the Assembly sent De Witt as a delegate to the Continental Congress. He then served on the state assembly from 1781 to 1786. As busy as he was, he still found time back at home to edit and publish the newspaper the *Ulster Sentinel.*[37]

Children:
John Charles (1755–1833) married Cornelia Cantine.
Margaret (1758–1827) married Johannes Bruyn.

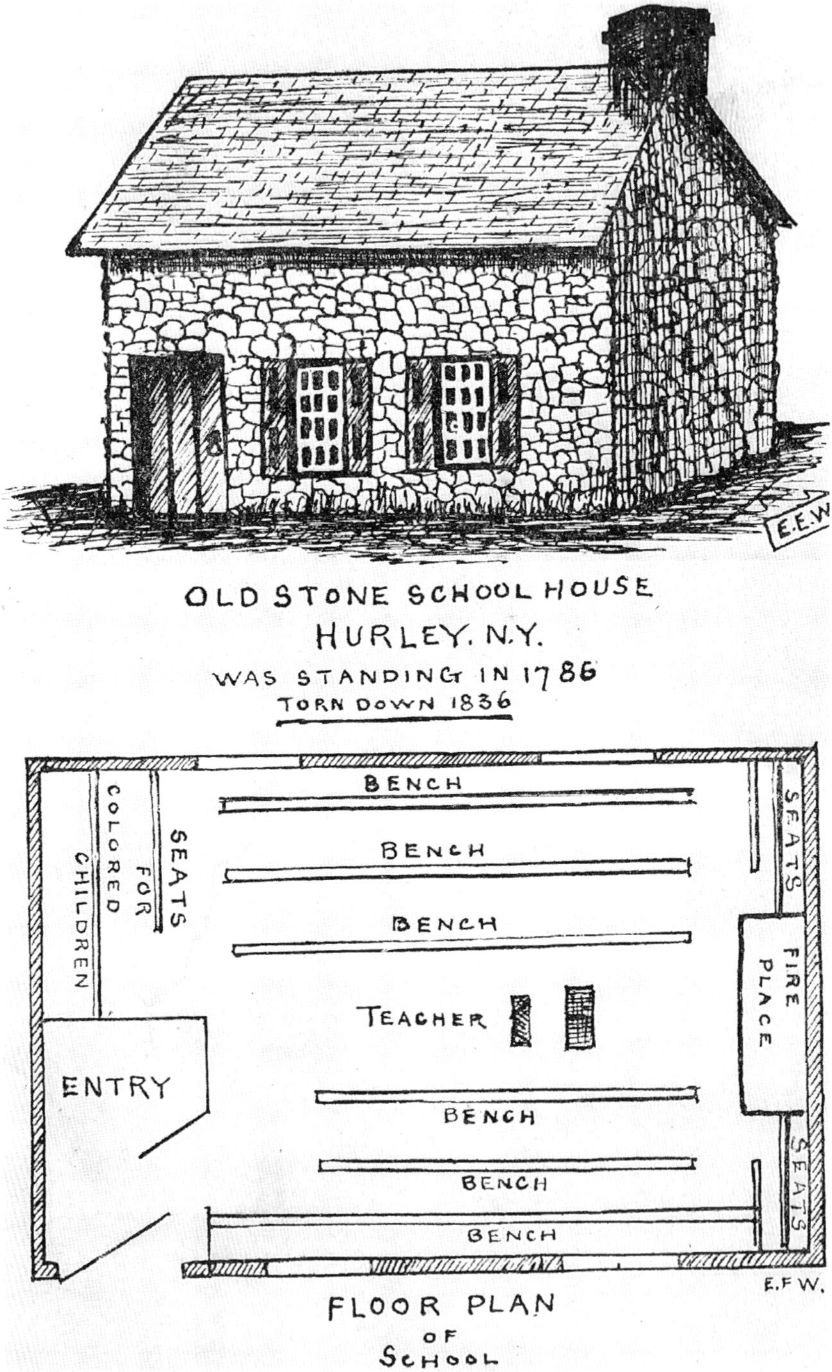

An illustration of the old stone schoolhouse on Main Street. *Courtesy of the Town of Hurley Historian's Office.*

Mary (1760–1798) married Jacobis Hasbrouck.
Gerritt (1762–1846) married Catherine Ten Eyck.
Ann (1764–?) married Peter Tappen.

Jan Van Deusen House

The name Van Deusen derived its origin from a small hamlet of about five hundred inhabitants in Noord Braband, Netherlands, called Deusen. Abraham Van Deusen had five sons who came to America about the middle of the seventeenth century. Their names were Isaac, Jacob, Melchert, Mattheus and Peter. Mattheus (Matthew), also listed as Travis, lived in Albany from 1657 to 1700. He married Helena (last name unknown) and had several children, including a son, Jan.

Jan married Maritie Van Buren in 1695 and had three children born at Claverack, Columbia County. Their son Jan was born in 1697 and raised in Kingston. In 1719, the younger Jan married Jan Roosa's youngest daughter, Hillegond, in Kingston.

By this time, all of Hillegond's older siblings were living on their own, including her brother, Aldert, who had purchased the house and property next door to her father's house from the Ostrander family. Jan Van Deusen moved in with Hillegond and her elderly parents. Her mother died about 1725 and was buried at the burial grounds behind their house. Her father remained in the home until his death in 1736. The house was then deeded to Jan Van Deusen by Jan Roosa's heirs. Like his father-in-law, Jan was a blacksmith. In 1715, he served under Captain Johannes Schepmoes in the Foot Company of the Hurley Militia. He was also a member of Captain Phillip Houghtaling's Light Horse Company in Kingston. In 1737, he served as surveyor of highways for the Town of Hurley. From 1738 to 1755, records show that he owned one slave. In 1741, Jan was a justice of the peace for Ulster County. He and Hillegond had five children; the oldest was Jan Van Deusen (Jr.), born in 1720.

At the age of eighteen, Jan Jr. began his long military career by joining the Hurley Militia foot company under Captain Cornelius Wynkoop. Three years later, in 1741, He married Wynkoop's daughter, Cornelia. She was the sister of Major Adrian and Colonel Cornelius Wynkoop.

A 1742 court record shows that Jan Jr. filed a complaint stating that he was slandered by Elizabeth Davenport. She had previously accused him of exposing himself to another young woman. Upon confrontation at a hearing concerning this complaint, Elizabeth recanted her story, stating that Jan had not exposed himself but instead had turned the woman around and offered to embrace her. Other witnesses backed up Van Deusen's claims, as well as his character, and the charge was dismissed.

In 1744, Jan Jr. obtained his father's property, took down the cottage and built the original rooms of the present stone house on the foundation of the Roosa house. He carved and dated his initials in the back of the house. Almost every owner of the house since that time has done the same.

As discontent grew among the colonists toward England, Van Deusen was moving up the military ladder. In October 1775, he was commissioned to Colonel Levi Pauling's regiment. Captain Jan Van Deusen was elected a deputy to the Provincial Congress, representing Hurley and Ulster County. In September 1776, at one of these meetings, "Capt John (Jan) Van Deusen says his whole [company], except his Lieutenant and himself are Tories."[38] It has been said that the citizens of Hurley were very supportive of the Revolutionary cause.

In October 1777, as the British cannons shelled Kingston's waterfront, the frightened residents fled the city. Among them were members of the Committee of Safety, who were in the process of forming a new state government. They took refuge in Hurley, staying in the local inns and at homes along with the troops of General George Clinton's army, which soon joined them from the south. Van Deusen offered his home as a meeting place for the committee, and the documents were hidden in a secret room in the attic. The room is now open to the upstairs, but the hidden door to access it still exists in a closed pantry in the kitchen.

The committee met here from October to November, making the Van Deusen House the temporary capitol building of New York State. The committee left for several reasons, including the inability to keep the meeting room warm enough. Some stories state that Van Deusen even brought in another stove, but to no avail.

Jan Jr. used his military connections and obtained many blacksmithing jobs from the local militias. In February 1778, he was reappointed quartermaster for the First, or Northern, Regiment of Ulster County. He continued serving and was appointed adjutant in 1779 under Abraham A. Hasbrouck. He was reassigned as lieutenant of levies in 1781 and was paymaster in Pawling's regiment from 1780 until 1781.

Jan Jr. and Cornelia had four daughters and a son. Jan married his second wife, Rachel (last name unknown), between the birth of his daughter Maria

The Van Deusen House on Main Street, early 1900s. *Courtesy of the Town of Hurley Historian's Office.*

in 1753 and the writing of his will in 1781. It is not known what happened to Cornelia or to Jan Jr.'s son, who disappears from the records before his father's death in 1801. The house was inherited by his daughter Maria, who married Henry De Witt in 1815. Henry sold the house to John C. Krom of Esopus. It then passed to his son, Samuel Krom, who deeded it to his daughters, Sarah M. Wynkoop and Jane, and Jane's husband, James P. Ten Eyck. In March 1864, the three sold the house and lot for $4,000 to Abraham Ten Eyck.

The LeFevre House

Matthew LeFevre served as a lieutenant and then captain of the Third Regiment of the Ulster County Militia. Four sons served with him during the Revolution. Matthew built several stone houses in the area for his sons, three of whom married Adam Swart's daughters. The LeFevres and Van Wagenens are related by marriage.

LeFevre built this house for his oldest son, Captain Simon LeFevre (1744–?), who served in the Revolution. Simon married Janneke Swart,

The LeFevre House in Wagendale, circa 2001. *Courtesy of David Baker.*

daughter of Adam Swart and Helena Burhans. He was one of the first elders of the Bloomington Reformed Church. The house is located along Route 32 near the intersection of Taylor Street.

MATTHEW LEFEVRE (1710–?) is the son of Andre LeFevre and Cornelia Blanjean and grandson to Simon LeFevre, one of the New Paltz patentees. He married Margaret Bevier (1717–?), daughter of Samuel Bevier and Magdelena Blanjean, in 1737. She was the granddaughter of Louis Bevier, also one of the New Paltz patentees. In 1750, Matthew purchased seven hundred acres from the Van Wagenens. He built a stone house on the west side of Creek Locks Road, just north of the thruway overpass. In 1910, part of the house was taken down.

Winslow Homer in Hurley

In 1795, a second school was built on Hurley Mountain Road. Peter Brink rented the land to the school for five pounds the first year. This school became the school for District 6, covering all of the families living on the western side of the Esopus Creek. The building was used until 1866, when the district was absorbed into Hurley School District Four. In the 1870s, Winslow Homer used this building, then in private ownership, as the backdrop for at least one painting of rural life. The one most easily recognized as the old school is the building in *Snap the Whip*. The building, though the appearance has changed, still stands against the hill on Hurley Mountain Road.

Monies needed to operate schools were raised by subscription. The subscribers, usually the parents of school-age children, elected annually three prominent local men as school trustees. In 1805, the trustees were Cornelius Elting, Dr. Richard Ten Eyck and Peter P. Roosa.

Chapter Three

DEVELOPING THE WEST

Bluestone Turns to Cement

Bluestone

The beginning of the bluestone industry in Ulster County can be marked by the discovery of the stone by Silas Brainard in 1831 with the first quarry. Bluestone is densely compressed sandstone formed more than 350 million years ago. It is usually bluish gray in color and was first discovered in eastern New York and northeastern Pennsylvania. By 1850, there were quarries all over the county.

The Plank Road began as footpaths. When the use of wagons increased, something had to be done to prevent them from being stuck. Tannin, the bark of the hemlock tree, was used to turn rawhides into leather. After being stripped, the trees were left to decay in the forest. They were cut into planks and laid onto the dirt roads. The heavy traffic wore down the planks, and soon the planks were replaced with bluestone on the road from West Hurley to Kingston.

Elements of the Statue of Liberty, the Brooklyn Bridge and the White House, as well as many town and city sidewalks, were made from Catskill bluestone. Affluent residents used bluestone sidewalks to show their wealth; the bigger the piece of stone, the more expensive it was. In 1886, Frederick Vanderbilt ordered twenty slabs, each measuring twenty feet long, ten feet wide and twelve inches thick, for his mansion on Fifth Avenue.

A rock cut and the Ulster and Delaware Railroad station in old West Hurley, circa 1900. This area boomed with the bluestone industry. *Courtesy of Jonathan and Iris Oseas.*

A constant supply of immigrants took the short trip from New York City to Kingston. The Irish Potato Famine of 1846 sparked an influx of Irish immigrants. Between 1846 and 1851, more than one million Irish men and women came to the United States and Canada. Those who ventured to Kingston found plenty of work. The area was home to a growing bluestone industry, as well as the Rondout docks, where they could work on the Delaware and Hudson (D&H) Canal, numerous brick factories and cement mines. Stoney Hollow, Moray Hill, Jockey Hill and Morgan Hill were heavily populated by Irish immigrants.

As the bluestone industry grew, so did the communities around it. Shanty villages of workers and their families appeared next to the quarries. These communities became part of Woodstock, Jockey Hill, Stoney Hollow and West Hurley.

By the late 1800s, the areas of West Hurley, Glenford and Ashton were booming. The bluestone industry, which had greatly increased the local population, was at its peak, though it would soon decline. New York City residents flocked to the area every summer for vacation, and boardinghouses dotted every block. Though mostly farming communities, these areas contained several churches, schools, post offices, mills and various other trades. According to a gazetteer, this area was destined for greatness. However, things were about to change.

The Delaware and Hudson Canal

William and Maurice Wurts, brothers and dry goods merchants from Philadelphia, discovered outcroppings of anthracite coal. They knew that this coal would be a valuable commodity and could make them a lot of money. They needed to figure out a way to move the coal from its location near Carbondale, Pennsylvania, to the markets in Philadelphia and New York City.

In 1822, they hired Benjamin Wright to make a detailed survey of the possibilities for canal routes. They felt that a canal was the best option, since hauling the coal over the mountains by sled or other means was impractical. Wright produced a plan for a canal, projecting that it could be built for about $1.5 million. The Wurts brothers began to bring investors onboard, and the canal was built between 1825 and 1829.

A gravity railroad carried the coal over the Moosic Mountains from Carbondale, 17 miles to Honesdale. From there, the coal was loaded onto barges, and it traveled on the canal 108 miles to Eddyville at the Rondout Creek. The canal measured twenty-eight feet wide and four feet deep. The locks were much smaller. During the next eleven years, increased demand for coal required the canal to be enlarged three times. With theses enlargements, the barges could carry as much as 130 tons of coal.

By 1860, the canal traffic could not keep up with the amount of coal coming into Honesdale. Railroad tracks were being laid everywhere, and soon they led to Honesdale. From there, the canal company leased tracks that led to Albany, giving it access to the Hudson River. The canal company began to transport coal by rail. As rail transportation increased, canal traffic decreased. In 1899, the section of canal between Honesdale and Ellenville was abandoned. In 1901, the canal section between Ellenville and High Falls was abandoned. The section between High Falls and Eddyville continued until about 1906, during the cement industry's peak.[39]

Ice Harvesting

During the winter, there was no work in the quarries or on the farms. Many men turned to harvesting ice for income. Once the ice became nine inches thick, the snow was cleared and cuts were plotted. Horses pulled ice-plow cutters to cut the lines creating the blocks. Metal blades cut to the desired depth, and blocks were removed. Men collected ice from lakes and ponds, such as Temple's Pond in Ashton, and stored it in icehouses covered with sawdust until summer, when it was used to keep food cold. Harvesting ice was an extreme occupation with many hazards. Men wore whatever they could to protect themselves from the cold. They wore boots with cork soles to grip the ice. This remained a big industry on the Hudson River until the invention of the refrigerator.

ASHTON

Just up the hill from the Olive Branch Railroad station sat Ashton.

Moylan's Boardinghouse

Run by Joseph Moylan and his sister-in-law, Kate, the house could hold up to twenty-five boarders. Most of the time, these boarders were vacationers from New York City, many of whom would stay the summer. The Moylans

Moylan's Corners, the crossroads in Ashton, about 1905. *Courtesy of Eleanor Elting Arold.*

grew most of their own fruits and vegetables. Many of the boarders came back every year. The house was taken down and rebuilt on Temple's Pond, avoiding its destruction for the reservoir.

T.S. Lennox (1864–1951) was the son of John Lennox and Louisa Frances Adsit. Tecumseh Sherman Lennox grew up on a farm in Beaverkill. In 1895, he married Glenford schoolteacher Sarah Ida Sagendorf. In 1898, he was appointed Glenford postmaster. In 1900, he bought the Van Hovenburg farmhouse in Ashton and built a store. In 1902, he became Ashton postmaster and had the post office in his store. In 1910, he purchased property in Glenford outside the future Reservoir area. In 1913, he had a large store built on the state road bordering his property. He rented the rooms above the store to a family. He asked the post office inspector what he should do about the Ashton post office (now under the water) and was told to do what he pleased. Since the original Glenford post office had closed in 1908, he decided to reopen the Ashton post office under the name Glenford. The name was officially changed on November 13, 1913, and Lennox remained postmaster. In the fall of 1914, the store/post office burned. Lennox moved the post office to his kitchen. In 1929, Lennox built another store on State Route 28, not far from the site of the old one.

Glenford

The original name of the village was Beaverkill. It received its first post office in 1887, and the name changed to Glenford. The Ohayo and Glenford mountains border the village, and many people built homes on the mountainsides. These homes were saved from destruction; others were not so lucky. John G. Baker was a farmer, quarryman and first postmaster of Glenford. His son, Byron, had a quarry, a charcoal kiln at Clapper Hollow and a sawmill. John Lennox had a grocery store and was a postmaster of Glenford.

The Henry Johnson and Sarah Brower Johnson home is one of the oldest in Glenford. It is located on the Glenford–Wittenberg Mountain Road, which was once part of the Ulster and Delaware Turnpike. This road connected farms in Delaware County to roads leading to Kingston. In the late 1800s, farmers would drive their herds of cattle and flocks of turkey down this road to the Kingston markets. Occasionally, they would stay overnight at the Johnson house. This house is also referred to as the Davidson Homestead and is the oldest house built almost entirely by women because the men were all off to war.

Greenwood Centenary ME Church

The church was built in 1865 and became the Glenford ME Church. It was locally known as the Beaverkill Church. The little red schoolhouse sat just behind it. Wesley Johnston gave the land for both of these buildings. He owned land up "dark hollow." When the Ulster and Delaware Railroad was moved to make way for the reservoir, the cut through a rock for the tracks led through the church. The railroad and New York City shared ownership. Julia Johnston, wanting to save the church, donated land to move the church. They hired John Crispell of Hurley to move it. The trustees received permission from railroad officials and a reservoir engineer to make the move. The engineer also told them that they did not have to go to Carlton Davis, the head engineer, for further permission. After the church

The Glenford schoolhouse (left) and the Glenford ME Church. *Courtesy of Eleanor Elting Arold.*

was moved, Davis reported it to the New York City Board of Water Supply. The board, in turn, took the church trustees to court for stealing the church. In December 1914, the verdict went in the board's favor. The church was ordered to pay forty-five dollars.

Old Hurley

Stone Dutch Reformed Church
Main Street

In 1801, after years of having to travel to Kingston for services, a petition signed by Cornelius Cole and fifty-seven others was approved to create a Dutch Reformed Church in Hurley. Soon after, residents constructed a single-room, two-story stone building halfway down Main Street next to the current museum. Dressed stones bearing the names of the prominent churchmen were placed on the front face of the church. The church had a hip roof and a tall, eight-sided steeple. A copper bell and a rooster weather vane hung in the belfry. The church was very large and the steeple very high—so high, in fact, that the neighbors were afraid of it falling on them. There were two rows of windows on the sides and two over the doorways. The large doors opened to the galleries. From this hall, two smaller doors opened into the main church, with two center aisles leading to the pulpit. This platform was very high and had a small set of stairs on either side forming a circular disc surrounding the preacher. The Reverend Thomas G. Smith served as the first pastor from 1801 until 1807.

On the left were benches for the elders—Matthew Ten Eyck, Petrus Roosa, Johannes Suylant and Cornelius Elting. The benches on the right were for the deacons—Petrus Elmendorf, Petrus Du Bois, Jeremiah Houghtaling and Cornelius Cole Jr. The general congregation purchased their benches filling the center of the hall. A persistently growing crack in the east wall caused the church consistory—made up of Reverend Benjamin C. Lippincott; Elders Christopher Newkirk, Solomon Shears, Benjamin A. Newkirk and Caleb M. Merritt; and Deacons Gerrit N. Roosa, James P. Ten Eyck, John M. Myer and William S. Elting—to purchase the Crispell Farm at the end of Main

An illustrative sketch of the Hurley stone church on Main Street. *Courtesy of the Town of Hurley Historian's Office.*

Street. The barn on the property was moved, and the minister moved into the Crispell House. By 1853, the stone church no longer existed. The old bell was sold to the congregation in West Hurley, and the timbers were either sold or used in the new church.[40]

Hurley Reformed Church
Main Street

In April 1853, a bid from John Palen of Stone Ridge for $2,800 was accepted for construction of the new church. The contract did not include the basement, which was built by John M. Myer Jr. for $340. In 1854, the new wood-frame church was built on the barn's vacant foundation. Stones from the old church were used to reinforce the new foundation and as the retaining wall of the new Hurley cemetery on Zandhoek Road.

Before the addition was added in 1957, there was a long shed with stalls for the horses facing the parsonage. A second shed faced the first. When cars replaced horses, the sheds served as parking stalls. The interior of the church has changed little. In the back of the church were two coal stoves, each measuring three feet across and five feet high. The pews are original. They were once numbered and leased to families in the congregation. Seventy dollars plus an annual seven-dollar fee got you the pew forever, and no one else could use it. The wealthy even had nameplates put on the pew door. The church was lit by a kerosene chandelier. The present chandelier and wall sconces were created by the Waligurski family of the Patentee Lighting Company. The church has operated in this building ever since.

Hurley Mountain Inn
Intersection of Old Route 209 and Wynkoop Road

Constructed in 1830 by Peter P. Wynkoop, this is the oldest continuously operated inn in the village. It was the stage stop on the Kingston–Ellenville line until the early 1900s, when the stage ceased operations. In 1837,

The Hurley Reformed Church at its present location on Main Street, circa 1900. *Courtesy of the Town of Hurley Historian's Office.*

The Hurley Mountain Inn in the early 1900s. *Courtesy of George K. Van Sickle.*

Peter became the first village postmaster and located the post office on the first floor. This remained the post office until it was moved to Main Street in 1853.

The first floor of the inn contained public rooms, while the second floor contained hotel rooms. During the summers of 1872 and 1873, Winslow Homer stayed at the inn and painted Esopus Valley landscapes. It is also believed that he had an interest in a local schoolteacher, whom he included in his paintings. In 1888, a suspension bridge was constructed next to the inn crossing the Esopus Creek. The inn's name became the Suspension Bridge House; in 1910, it became the Hurley Hotel. Locals refer to it as the Hurley Hilton. In 1982, the bar scenes in the movie *Tootsie* were filmed here.

The property sits where the Mill Brook and Esopus Creek meet on Marbletown Road (Old 209).

In a deed dated May 1710,[41] Charles Viley and his wife sold this mill lot to William Clarke and his wife. It mentions a town gate blocking the approach from Marbletown across the road where the Mill Kill (Brook) crosses.

The old suspension bridge spanned the Esopus Creek until the 1930s, when the current iron bridge was installed. The abutments from the old bridge are still visible from the creek.

O&W Railroad

The Ontario and Western (O&W) Railroad connected areas from as far south as New Jersey northwest to Oswego, New York, on Lake Ontario. A branch line completed in 1902 ran from Kingston to Ellenville, New York, including a stop at the station in Hurley. Passengers who came into Kingston on the O&W and wished to continue to New York City had to take a trolley from the Kingston station downtown to the line going to the city, and vice versa. Passenger traffic flourished until the 1930s. Coal, feed, fertilizer and the mail also came into the station, and corn, milk and other farm products were sent out. For a time, high school students used the train to go to school in Kingston.

Sometime in the early 1930s, passenger traffic traveled on a single Brill motorcar, which operated between Kingston and Summitville. Brill car #804 was the last to operate on the O&W, and it ran on the Kingston Branch. It made the last passenger run out of Kingston on September 5, 1940. The following year, some Sunday specials ran from Kingston to Accord. The other O&W lines operated until 1950.

The Route 209 bridge was originally built when the railroad was constructed. Railroad Avenue led from Main Street behind the railroad depot and crossed the tracks to Wynkoop Road. When the railroad was replaced by Route 209, Depot Road replaced Railroad Avenue and dead-ended instead of crossing the road. Eventually, in the 1950s, the rail branch was no longer used, and the O&W station was destroyed to make room for the new Route 209 to be built.

The O&W station depot at Hurley. The Dr. Richard Ten Eyck House is on the left. *Courtesy of Chester Hartfield.*

Zandhoek School

In 1836, the school commissioners decided that the schoolhouse on Main Street needed to be replaced. They purchased a lot on Main Street, now Zandhoek Road. They built a larger one-room schoolhouse on the lot, with the front door at the back side of the building. Heat was provided by a coal stove at the center of the building. In 1872, a second-story wood addition was added to the school for its growing population. The lower grades were taught on the ground floor, with the upper grades upstairs.

Students attended first through eighth grade. If their families wished them to further their education, the student would attend the Kingston Academy on the Academy Green to complete what is now a high school education. During the 1800s, more girls than boys attended the Kingston Academy because the boys were needed at home to help with the family farm.

Charles Gerrit De Witt (1789–1839) was the son of Gerrit and grandson of Charles De Witt. He began by studying and practicing law and soon became a clerk for the Navy Department. He then followed in

The Zandhoek School facing Main Street. The Houghtaling House is on the right. *Courtesy of Ruth Lord.*

his grandfather's footsteps in two ways: he was elected to the Twenty-first Congress in 1829, and he was editor of the *Ulster Sentinel*. In 1833, President Andrew Jackson appointed him the Charge d'Affaires (now called an ambassador) to Central America. After his return, he took a boat up the Hudson. As it passed Newburgh, Charles committed suicide.

AUGUST KAUSS (1843–1913) was born in Germany. His parents are not known. He immigrated to the United States in 1859. Shortly after his arrival, he enlisted in Company D, Eighth New York Infantry Division. He was mustered out sometime in 1863 and reenlisted in Company H, Fifteenth New York, Heavy Artillery Division. Both units were formed in New York City. The heavy artillery unit was created to man military forts during the Civil War, but since there were more military units than forts, it saw action in the war as infantry.

In April 1865, at the Battle of Five Forks, Virginia, August captured a Rebel battle flag. Since this was an important feat during the war, he was awarded the Medal of Honor. He was discharged from service on August 22, 1865.

He came to West Hurley between 1900 and 1905 and rented a house. By 1910, he had moved to Old Hurley, where he rented a house on Roosa Lane. He died of a stroke on April 27, 1913, without any known relatives. He was buried at the new Hurley Cemetery in an unmarked grave until a veterans' organization inquired about his burial. Ike Roosa, caretaker of the cemetery, located the grave, and they marked the site with the present federal marker.

Locally, the story is told that August gave his family Bible and his medal and other personal effects to Ike Roosa, who was his neighbor on Roosa Lane, for safekeeping. Ike stored these items in his barn. When he and his wife decided to go on their first vacation, a fire completely destroyed the barn and all of its contents.

GEORGE P NEWKIRK (1820–1901) was born the free son of slave Dianna Johnson. Her master was a Newkirk, and thus he took his surname. In 1843, he obtained work as a farm laborer in Hurley. In 1850, he purchased land from Cornelius P. Wyncoop on Hurley Mountain Road just south of Dug Hill Road. The property cost twelve dollars, and he built a house for his wife, Margaret, and their three children. They eventually had twelve children, but only five survived. This is the first record of an African American purchasing land in Hurley, and within three years, he had purchased three more parcels to add to his original parcel.

George dammed a stream on his property creating a freshwater pond. He established a business selling fresh clams. He stored the clams in the pond until they were sold. Later, he became the village caterer for weddings and funerals.

Part of George's property went up along the Hurley Mountain. Before and during the Civil War, it is said that he provided temporary shelter for traveling black families. Local residents have unearthed many artifacts from this time period, and perhaps George was a part of the Underground Railroad. The Hurley area has many stories of various houses being stops for the runaway slaves on their way north.

George's eldest son served with the 125th Artillery for the Northern Army. He died in combat in 1866 and was buried in Hurley near his father's property. Being educated, a landowner and of some wealth earned George the right to vote. He became the first black to vote, not only in Hurley, but also in New York State. He died in his home and was buried next to his son.

Old West Hurley

The Methodist Episcopal Church of West Hurley

Beginning in 1843, Methodist services were originally held at the schoolhouse and private residences. The congregation was officially incorporated in 1850 with twenty members. Henry Sax and Edward Van Steenburgh presided over the election of John R. Lewis, Alexander Carnweiht and Edward Van Steenburgh as trustees. The first church was built in 1853, and when it became too small, another was built in 1868. Reverend John Davies served as the first pastor.[42]

In 1881, a large shed was added to shelter the horses and wagons. Stoves originally sat on the main floor of the church but were later installed downstairs.

In March 1910, New York City Water purchased the church and about six acres of property for $8,500. In 1913, the church trustees purchased property from John and Sara Groves. New construction began in September. Many items from the old church were used in the new one, including the memorial stained-glass windows, the pews and the pulpit.

The corner of Main and Honey Streets in West Hurley circa 1900. It possibly shows the J. C. Hardenburgh House. *Courtesy of Jonathan and Iris Oseas.*

In 1928, a lightning bolt struck the tower of the church, setting off a fire that eventually claimed the entire church. Residents of West Hurley were able to save several items, including a stained-glass memorial window, the organ and pews. A metal roof delayed the rapidly spreading fire, but the high winds fed the flames and spread embers. Only the heavy rain protected nearby buildings. A pumper tanker from the Wiltwyck station in Kingston was no match for the fire, and lack of a local water source did not help. In the end, only the foundation remained. Hobart Rowe received the contract to rebuild, using the few saved items. The congregation purchased a bell from a closed Presbyterian church in Jefferson, New York. Services began again in 1929.

A new church bell was purchased in Holland for the Hurley Dutch Reformed Church, and the congregation gave it to the West Hurley church. West Hurley, in turn, gave it to the Lutheran Church of Woodstock. In 1943, the West Hurley church celebrated its 100th anniversary. In 1993, due to decades of lingering numbers and competition from two other churches, the administration voted to become the Reservoir United Methodist Church. In 2001, the church closed its doors for the last time.

Reformed Church of West Hurley

This church was first organized in 1848 by Reverend Alexander Gulick with a membership of twenty-five. The first church was built in 1854. A second church was removed to the village in 1870.

St. John's Roman Catholic Church

This church was formed and built in 1857. In 1869, a new church was built for $10,000.

Olive Branch

Olive Branch was one of the hamlets razed by the reservoir project. All residents were displaced. It served as the train station on the Ulster and Delaware Railroad for the towns of Ashton and Olive Branch. If still in existence, the tracks would run straight through the middle of the reservoir from east to west.

The villages were surrounded by Big and Little Toinje Mountains, Tysteneyck Mountain and Markle Heights. The valley was made up of swamp, woods, pasture, quarries, open fields and the Beaverkill Creek. The station agent was Joseph Furman.

Henry C. Bush ran a saloon and grocery store in Olive Branch. He was the Ashton postmaster in 1894. De Witt Ballard and his family ran a commissary and a boardinghouse for foreign reservoir workers. Cornelius McAulliffe was a teamster. He died during one of his trips delivering stone to the docks. James Mulligan was a quarryman, farmer and blacksmith. Richard Smith was the first postmaster of Ashton, appointed in 1886. Sidney Pearson was a Wintergreen distiller and farmer. Fred Hale was a farmer, quarryman, farmer and carpenter. Henry Berryman was a shoemaker. The Henry Boyce House was taken down by William Johnson and rebuilt on the Glenford–Wittenberg Road. These are just a sample of the people who were uprooted from their homes in Ashton and Olive Branch.

Olive Branch Methodist Episcopal Church

The first church was built in 1866. In 1913, it joined with the Shokan church to form the Ashokan ME Church. T.S. Lennox bought the building for $600 and tore it down. The pulpit furnishings went to the Ashokan ME Church, the pews were sold and two large six- by twelve-foot bluestones went to the new Lennox home in Glenford to be used for the porch.

Rosendale

This village was formed on April 26, 1844, from parts of the towns of Hurley, New Paltz and Marbletown. A "dale" is a valley, and the name Rosendale was used as early as 1702 to designate the valley where the current village lies along the Rondout Creek. The residents living in this area were isolated from the other three villages and desired their own village.

Sojourner Truth

Isabella Hardenburgh was born about 1797 as a slave in the home of Colonel Johannis Hardenburgh in the town of Hurley, now Rosendale. Johannis died when she was an infant, and she and her parents were bequeathed to his son, Charles Hardenburgh. When Charles died in 1806, Isabella's parents were freed, being of advanced age. The remainder of his estate was auctioned off, including his slaves. At that point, Isabella was only about nine and not yet valuable. She was sold, along with a flock of sheep, to John Neely. Isabella, who only spoke Dutch, did not get along with Mrs. Neely, who only spoke English. Mrs. Neely would whip Isabella because she did not understand her.

In 1809, Martin Schryver, a fisherman and tavern keeper, purchased Isabella. He was kind to her, and when business was slow, he allowed her free time. In 1810, John Dumont, a wealthy landowner from New Paltz, purchased Isabella. Mrs. Dumont disliked Isabella and blamed her for things she did not do. Dumont married Isabella off to one of his elderly slaves named Tom. She bore five children for the Dumonts. They sold her five-

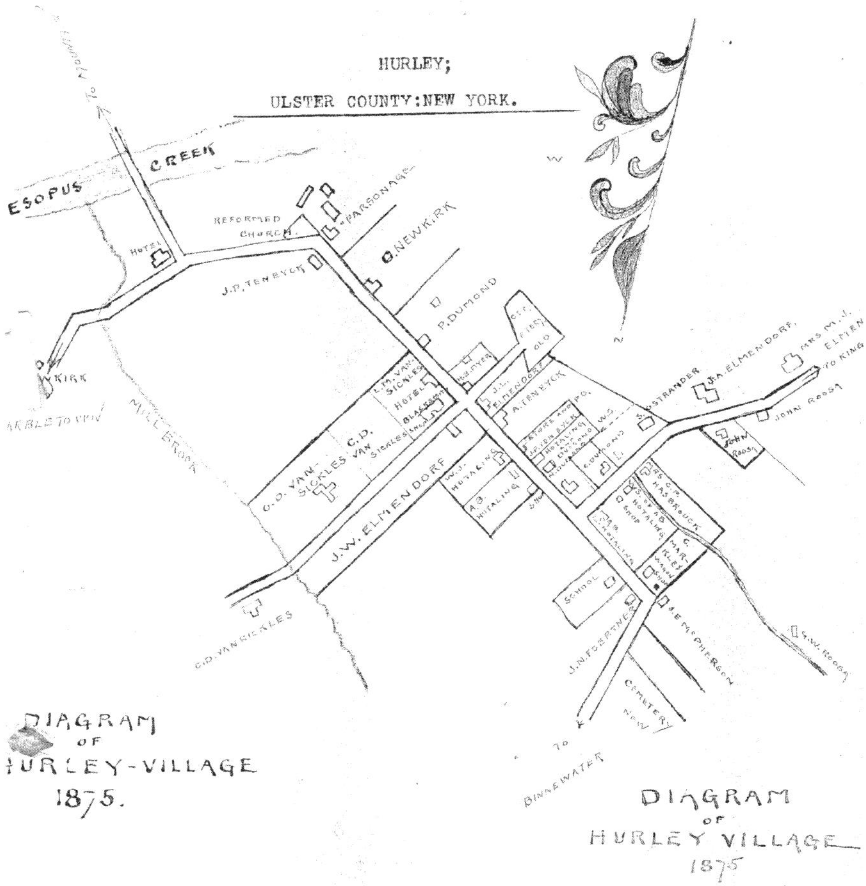

A diagram of Hurley Village in 1875 drawn by Dr. Richard Nash. *Courtesy of the Town of Hurley Historian's Office.*

year-old son, Peter, to the Gedney family in New Paltz. Solomon Gedney then sold him to his brother-in-law, who later gave him to his daughter in Alabama—a violation of New York State law.

In 1825, the Dumonts had promised Isabella her freedom, but they reneged. The following year, she ran away with her infant daughter to the home of Levi Roe, an abolitionist. He was ill, so he sent her to the home of Isaac and Maria Van Wagenen.

They took her in immediately. Dumont tracked down the runaways and demanded their return. However, Isaac offered to buy them. Dumont agreed, and they stayed with the Van Wagenens. During this time, Isabella worked for the Van Wagenens. They encouraged her to file a complaint with the courts to get her son Peter back. She filed a complaint against Gedney. Facing a fine and prison time, Gedney brought the boy back, and he was returned to Isabella.

On July 4, 1827, New York State law emancipated slaves. The Van Wagenens gave freedom to Isabella's daughter, who was not covered under the law.

In 1829, Isabella left for New York City, where she worked for the cause of "fallen women." She then joined the African Methodist Episcopal Zionist Church. In 1843, she heard God give her the name "Sojourner." She went to Brooklyn, where she met a Quaker woman who asked her name. When asked her last name, God told her "Truth." From then on, she used that name. She gave many lectures on the abolitionist movement and fought for women's rights. Sojourner moved to Battle Creek, Michigan, where she died in 1883.[43]

Chapter Four

HURLEY IN THE TWENTIETH CENTURY

The Ashokan Reservoir

The turn of the century brought about the beginning of many changes. Portland Cement was beginning to replace all other materials as a cheaper substitute for sidewalks and building materials. The bluestone industry had withered down to nothing. The very landscape of the West Hurley area was about to change forever. As shown throughout this book, the Esopus Creek played an active role in the livelihood of the town of Hurley. In the late 1800s, New York City was growing at a rapid rate. More water was needed to supply the growing city. In the 1900s, New York State water commissioners came to the area and decided that it would be the ideal location for a new dam and reservoir. With the ink still wet on the paperwork, test borings were taken at Bishop's Falls located in Olive Branch to determine the depth of the bedrock. Once the final decision was made, local residents were given ten days to sell their houses to New York City or lose them. Compensation for property was low, and landowners sued. Some lawsuits lasted for twenty-five years.

Moylan's Corners was the crossroads of Ashton about 1905. The Esopus Valley contained small farms, bluestone quarries, schools, churches and post offices. The Ulster and Delaware Railroad brought residents from New York City to the large boardinghouses for the summer. It cost about seven dollars a month for a room and meals. Moylan's was one of many boardinghouses

A view of the lower basin taken from a bridge over the hate chamber. *Courtesy of Eleanor Elting Arold.*

Moylan's Boardinghouse at Moylan's Corners in Ashton. *Courtesy of Eleanor Elting Arold.*

in the area. It was located across the street from the Lennox store and post office. With the threat of destruction by the new Ashokan Reservoir, the house was dismantled and rebuilt on the eastern end of Temple's Pond. It is still in use today.

A great deal of heavy equipment was brought in to the area for the reservoir project, including steam shovels, steamrollers, stone crushers and concrete mixers. Small eight- to twelve-ton steam locomotives, called dinkeys, engines and 117 dump cars were brought in from New York City to move equipment from one construction site to another on four and a half miles of track.

There was a daily workforce of about thirty-five hundred men. The majority were common laborers earning $1.20 a day for an eight-hour shift. Stonemasons earned about $3.00 a day, powder men earned $10.00 a week and water boys made $1.00 a day. Most workers stayed in company dormitories costing $20.00 or more a month, and they bought the overpriced food in the commissary. Most of the workers were African American and Italian immigrants, many just off the boats in New York City.

The L.E. Du Mond General Merchandise Store sat at the corner of Main Street and Railroad Avenue and was established by George Stewart and Levi Du Mond in 1895. In 1905, Levi Du Mond bought out George Stewart, his brother-in-law, and became sole proprietor. Whole families came looking for work at the reservoir. Those who lived in camps outside the

The L.E. Du Mond General Merchandise Store at the corner of Main Street and Railroad Avenue. *Courtesy of Jonathan and Iris Oseas.*

main housing area did their shopping in the local towns. The Italian camp, for example, purchased all of its living supplies from the L.E. Du Mond General Merchandise Store.

Reservoir workers completed the large dam on June 4, 1912 . The main dam was mostly made of concrete, 192 feet thick at the bottom, 26.4 feet thick at the top, 252 feet high and 1,000 feet long. Many skeptics felt that this dam would never hold.

New York Boulevard was the main road used during and after construction of the reservoir. It ran forty miles around the reservoir and crossed it at the Dividing Weir. However, the work was far from over. The next step was to clear the basin of all vegetation, houses, cemeteries and leftover contents of outhouses. This would help guarantee the purity of the water going to New York City.

Water would soon fill the quarries, and villages would either disappear or move for survival.

The Glenford church after it was moved. *Courtesy of Eleanor Elting Arold.*

To most people, the reservoir is a beautiful area where many locals love to fish. It is the oldest city-owned reservoir in the Catskill Mountains. At its maximum length, it is twelve miles; its maximum width is one mile. It can hold up to 123 billion gallons of water. It is surrounded by relocated communities, Route 28 and Route 28A. Reservoir Road crosses through the middle at the causeway. The water flows down the reservoir to Olive Branch, where it enters the Catskill Aqueduct and flows ninety-two miles to the Kensico Reservoir just north of the Bronx. Not only were several hamlets relocated, but also over one thousand residents, more than twenty-five cemeteries (including the bodies), roads, farms, bluestone quarries and homes were moved. It changed the landscape of the towns of Hurley, Olive and Marbletown forever and has been a great source of contention between the downstream communities and New York City.

William Saxe bought two large parcels of land, one creating the new hamlet of West Hurley and the other called Riverside, located on the now Old Route 209 along the Esopus Creek, just south of Old Hurley. Not long after the move, there was an Ulster and Delaware Railroad station at Glenford on property formerly owned by Wallace Lee.

Old Hurley

Boy Scouts

Troop 20 was the first Boy Scout Troop established in Hurley on November 19, 1937. The Hurley Reformed Church sponsored them, with meetings at the church on Fridays. Carl F. Scherick, of West Hurley, was the first scoutmaster, and William Herdenburgh, of Hurley, was his assistant scoutmaster. The committee included G. Chesterfield, chairman; O.D.B. Ingalles; R.H. Loughan; Leland W. Ten Eyck; Chester Chiten; and J. Leonard Lockwood.

The troop was active until 1946. Between then and 1953, it was inactive, except for the year 1950, with Henry A. Goldman as scoutmaster. In 1954, John V. Kemble Jr. restarted the troop as scoutmaster, and it has been active ever since. The first Boy Scouts were Robert G. Brown, John R. Harder, George Malsom, Robert Merker, Peter Palen, Walter G. Piltz, Edward Slater, James Winchall and Elbert Laughram.

Hurley Fire Department

In July 1942, the Fred B. Ballard Pencil Factory burned to the ground leaving little more than a small concrete storage area standing. Local residents fought the fire using a bucket brigade of milk buckets, and fire trucks from Kingston were called to help. What began as a small bathroom fire became the birth of the Hurley Fire Department. After the fire, the process was started to form the department. By April 1943, everything was in place, and officers and commissioners were elected. They were Chief Lawrence Beutner, Assistant Chief Harry Battenfeld, Captain William Markle, Foreman Joseph Armstrong, President Arthur Nash, Vice-President Otis Tracey and Secretary/Treasurer Paul Weber. The first board of commissioners consisted of Chairman Justin Bell, Lowell Brooks, Fred Robison, Lyman Schoonmaker, Treasurer W.G. Burhans and Secretary Minard Elmendorf. Regular meetings began in May, and the fire company was born with twenty-five charter members. In June, the first fire truck was put into service and stored at Merkle's garage, the first fire station. This building still exists as the Hurley Country Store.

Hurley School

By the late 1930s, the Zandhoek School had become too small and worn out after one hundred years of use. The school trustees purchased two parcels of land between Millbrook Avenue and Schoolhouse Lane for $40,000 and built a new elementary school named the Hurley School. The first classes were held in the fall of 1939. The original building consisted of four classrooms on the main floor and a multipurpose room in the basement. The first year there were seventy-five students from the first to eighth grades.

The Zandhoek School was sold to a private individual and eventually taken down. The top story was taken down as one unit and placed on a foundation just to the left of the old school foundation. Today, it is a private residence, although the attic still shows traces of its original use. The stone walls of the first floor were removed and the cellar hole was filled in. Only the faint outline of the covered basement walls show where the building once stood.

As classroom space was needed, the Hurley Town Hall, now the library, was used. Four more classrooms were added in 1955 and two more rooms in 1957. A driveway connecting Schoolhouse Lane and Millbrook Avenue provided access to the school. After 1957, the voters elected not to enlarge the school again. When needed, the eighth and sometimes seventh grades were sent to Kingston schools for instruction, and the cafeteria would be closed and used as a classroom. In the early 1960s, another addition was built, adding several more classrooms and a gymnasium and stage. It is now called the Ernest C. Myer School after its longtime teacher and principal.

Dr. Richard Nash and his wife, Carrie, purchased the Van Deusen House in 1906. They had no children. As a young man, he worked for the U.S. government in Munich, Germany, inspecting immigrants bound for the United States. He later worked in New York City as a public health worker. He became interested in the city's history and published articles in *Historical Guide to the City of New York*.

He then moved to Hurley and focused on local history. He collected historical documents and published articles in *Olde Ulster*, a monthly magazine featuring local history and genealogy, under the name "the Doctor." He also created a large glass-plate photo collection of Hurley's houses and other historic local buildings.

After his death, his wife sold all of this to a collector, who in turn donated it to the New York Historical Society in New York City, where it can be viewed today.

C.G. Hine, in his book *The Old Mine Road*, mentions meeting with a doctor in Hurley who took him around the town. Hine remarks on the house and how Dr. Nash had modernized it. Most of the building remains the same today.

"New" West Hurley

West Hurley School #2

The West Hurley one-room schoolhouse was built in 1913 on the corner of Wall and Cedar Streets. The first trustee was Harry White, an artist from Woodstock, but Mrs. Clayton Vredenbutgh took over. When more room was needed, the school rented a room in Norman Cole's house on

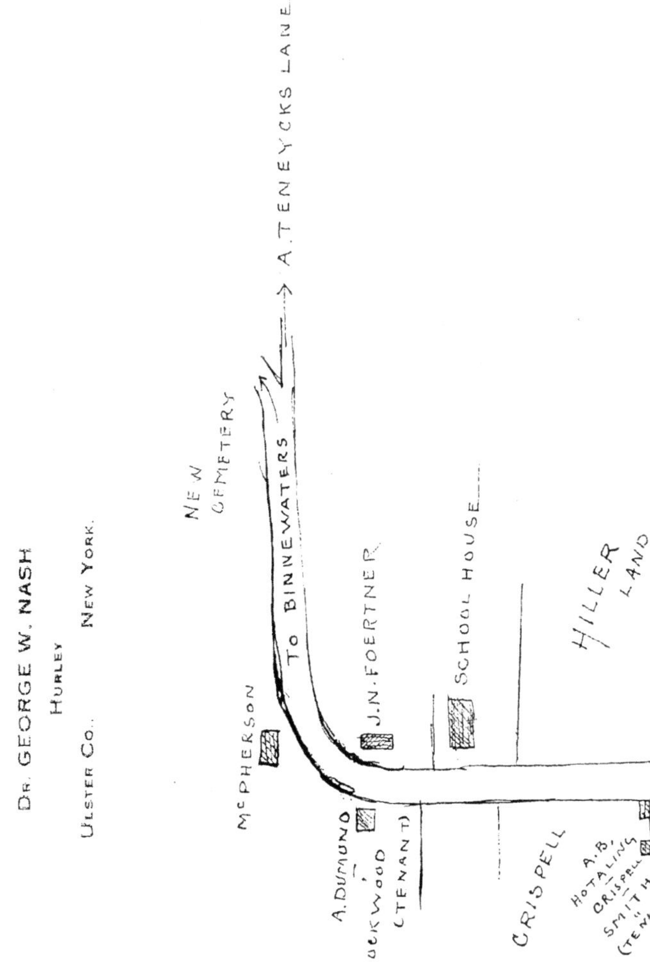

An illustration of Hurley landmarks created by Dr. Richard Nash in the early 1900s. *Courtesy of the Town of Hurley Historian's Office.*

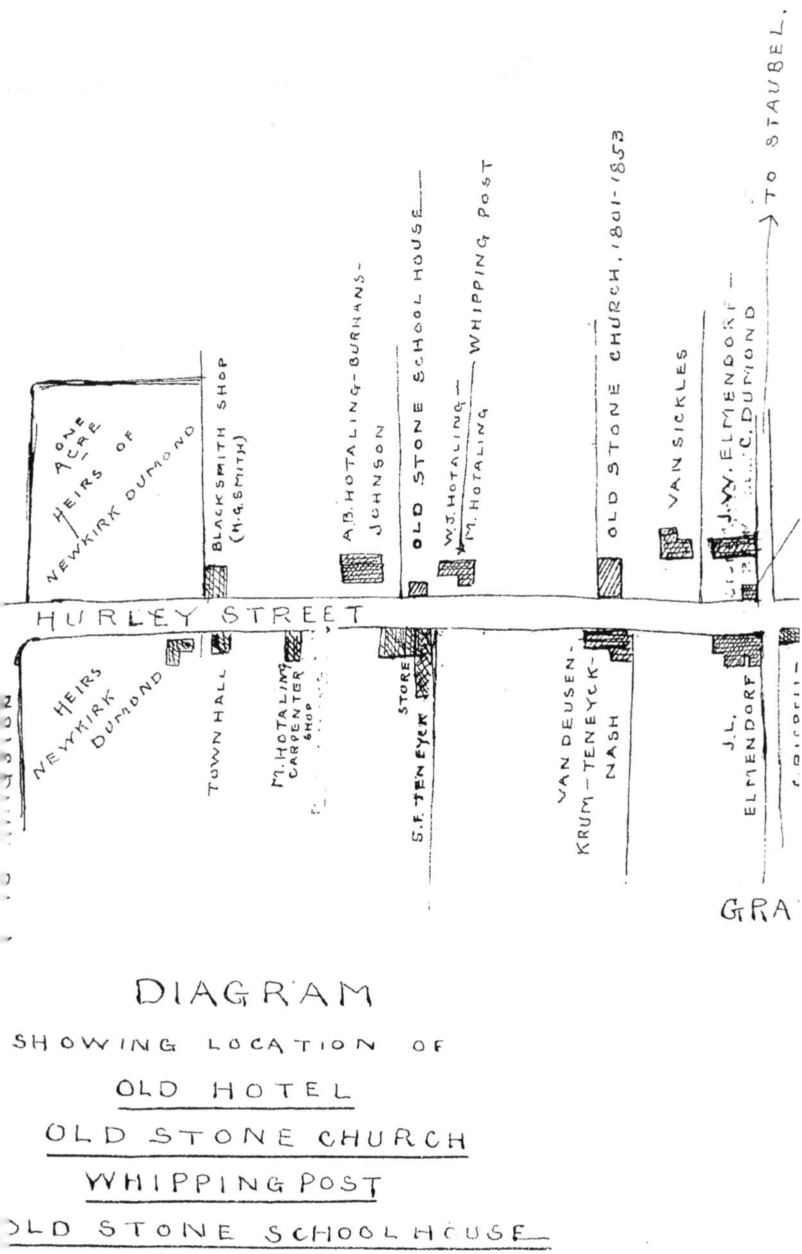
HURLEY STREET
ONE ACRE
HEIRS OF NEWKIRK DUMOND
BLACKSMITH SHOP (H.G.SMITH)
A.B. HOTALING - BURHANS - JOHNSON
OLD STONE SCHOOL HOUSE
W.J. HOTALING - M. HOTALING
WHIPPING POST
OLD STONE CHURCH, 1801 - 1853
VAN SICKLES
J.W. ELMENDORF - C. DUMOND
TO STAUBEL.
HEIRS NEWKIRK DUMOND
TOWN HALL
M. HOTALING CARPENTER SHOP
STORE
S.F. TEN EYCK
VAN DEUSEN - KRUM - TENEYCK - NASH
J.L. ELMENDORF
GRA
DIAGRAM
SHOWING LOCATION OF
OLD HOTEL
OLD STONE CHURCH
WHIPPING POST
OLD STONE SCHOOLHOUSE

Route 28. It then rented a room from John Saxe on Cedar Street. In 1936, construction on a new two-room schoolhouse began behind the old school. Students moved into the new school in 1938. The principal was Ernest Myer. He taught grades five through eight, and Irene Guff taught the younger grades. A kindergarten was added, and classes were held in the West Hurley Methodist Church. In 1961, the school added four classrooms, a stage, an office, cafeterias and a kitchen. Because of overcrowding, two more rooms were added in 1962.

Morgan Hill School #8

According to a letter from Arlene Smith Sheeley, she attended this school from 1936 to 1944. Eva Hess was the teacher there for many years. There was no running water; nor were there indoor bathrooms. There was a coal stove in the back, and a janitor who lived nearby took care of it. There was a piano in the back, and Mrs. Hess played two songs each morning. On Fridays, they had "music," which consisted of a box of wooden hammers, tambourines and triangles. There were no snow days. Mrs. Hess drove up with Mrs. Corrigan, who taught at the Stony Hollow School. The Stony Hollow School no longer exists.

Listed in a picture taken about 1942 are the following students: George Beesmer, Glenford Beesmer, Henry Beesmer, Richard Beesmer, Donald Beesmer, Roger Beesmer, Benjamin Winne, Mary Winne, Milton Winne, James Winne, Raymond Winne, William Hunnbeck, Walter Oehler, Clifton Longendyke, Carol Smith, Arlene Smith, Gertrude Franz, Marianna Houlihan, Thomas Houlihan, Lawrence Houlihan, Bernard Smith, Hazel Vente, Thomas Vente, Henry Gleich and William Oehler.

In 1939, the trustees of the district schools voted to add single-seat chemical toilets to the school. Irene Guff retired in 1940, and Mrs. William Russell took over. Ernest Myer left in 1941 to become principal of the new Hurley school. Mrs. Russell took over as principal. In 1953, the school added a new oil stove and flush toilets. In May 1955, the trustees considered sending the students to the Onteora schools. In June, School Districts One, Five and Eight were urged to consolidate. James McCarthy, principal of West Hurley, encouraged this consolidation, stating that if it was not done, they might lose control over the destiny of the local school system.

On May 7, 1957, Mrs. Rosa Goins read the order from the commissioner declaring the district part of the Onteora centralization beginning on June 30. Children who had finished their sophomore year at Kingston High School could finish at Kingston. Onteora paid their tuition and for transportation. In July 1969, the last West Hurley one-room school was closed. The District Six school located on Route 28A became part of the Onteora School District.

Appendix

NAMES AND DATES OF PEOPLE BURIED IN OLD HURLEY BURIAL GROUNDS

NAME	BIRTH	DEATH
De Witt, Colonel Charles	1727	August 27, 1787
Blandina, his wife	1731	November 4, 1765
Garret	August 8, 1762	February 5, 1846
Catherine Ten Eyck, his wife	October 27, 1765	April 3, 1840
Charles Garret	November 7, 1789	April 12, 1839
Maria Van Deusen, wife of Henry	September 9, 1755	May 29, 1813
Caty Newkirk, wife of Ten Eyck De Witt	November 24, 1793	March 12, 1822

NAME	BIRTH	DEATH
Crispell, John	January 14, 1764	September 24, 1842
Jane Hasbrouck, his wife	September 28, 1769	October 29, 1812
Abraham G.	July 12, 1799	March 12, 1823
Adaline M. Barber, wife of Abraham Elting Crispell	June 8, 1825	February 10, 1854
Peter, their son	October 5, 1850	December 27, 1852
Ira, their son	June 24,1853	July 5, 1854
Dr. Peter Jr.	August 3, 1794	December 19, 1878
Catharina Elting, his wife	March 23, 1795	March 9, 1857
Peter, son of Peter C. and Margaret	March 19, 1859	May 21, 1861
John P.	March 6, 1817	September 12, 1900
Gertrude Beetty, his wife	December 7, 1844	January 18, 1894
Du Mond, Cornelius	April 11, 1785	May 4, 1813
Blandina Crispell, his wife	July 29, 1797	June 12, 1860
John C.	1806	1863
Sally A. du Bois, his wife	1812	1871
Sarah, their daughter	1842	1917
John, their son	1845	1900
Peter, their son	1835	1895
Anthony D.	November 12, 1822	August 16, 1893
Maria Schoonmaker, his wife	April 4, 1827	March 4, 1870

Name	Birth	Death
Elmendorf, Margritje Crispell, wife of Johannis	April 8, 1766	January 27, 1850
Benjamin	December 2, 1834	May 26, 1895
George Washington, his son with Jane Coin	June 21, 1872	July 3, 1877
Annatje Du Mond, wife of Petrus	June 8, 1748	July 3, 1823
Benjamin	December 29, 1783	September 15, 1856
Eve Freer, his wife	July 4, 1802	May 29, 1894
Edgar	1827	1909
Mary V., his wife	May 4, 1830	July 21, 1856
Mary V., their daughter	July 16, 1856	June 1, 1886
Du Mond, Co. B, 120 Regt. NY	1814	February 5, 1877
Magdelina Elting, wife of Andrias	August 31, 1781	January 17, 1844
Catherine M.	June 11, 1818	October 5, 1841
Conrad	1725	August 1835
John R.	August 19, 1812	September 5, 1897
Willhelmus	November 12, 1786	August 13, 1859
Catherine Kiersted, his wife	February 21, 1789	December 20, 1887
Oscar	January 24, 1863	January 18, 1913
John P.	Unknown	Unknown
Jane, his wife	Unknown	Unknown
Philip, Co. B, 120 Regt. NYSV	September 10, 1819	March 15, 1879
Elizabeth Dewald, wife of Benjamin	1790	September 1825
John W.	1825	1903
Emaline, his wife	March 19, 1823	March 5, 1855
Susan Coin, his wife	1842	1919
Carrie, daughter of Silas and Emma	October 26, 1867	February 12, 1870

NAME	BIRTH	DEATH
Roosa, Abraham		
Gaasbeck, son of John and		
Margaret	1847	January 29, 1852
Roosa, Catherine	April 12, 1823	January 11, 1831
*Peter	November 4, 1824	January 15, 1825
*Charles H.	September 11, 1834	February 18, 1835
*Mynderson	July 2, 1836	April 22, 1837
*Peter A.	September 23, 1838	March 23, 1840
*Children of Andrew P. & Sarah Roosa		
Bernard, Arza	1867	Unknown
Nellie Crispell, his wife	1872	1909
Van Keuren, Jacob	November 26, 1786	May 13, 1868
Maria Van Vliet, his wife	February 1, 1795	November 12, 1867
Anne E.	November 29, 1850	December 27, 1870
Susan J.	April 30, 1884	December 17, 1868
James M.	October 25, 1820	May 22, 1890
Rebecca M. Ostrander,		
his wife	March 8, 1818	May 12, 1885
Susan	July 31, 1814	February 1, 1891
Selina, daughter of		
Alexander and Julia	January 18, 1851	February 18, 1853
Krom, Egbert B.		
Edmond H., Co. A,156	July 20, 1806	October 13, 1877
Reg. NY	1832	April 1, 1865
John G.	September 23, 1755	November 3, 1837
Jantje Swart, his wife	July 6, 1763	June 10, 1842
Samuel	December 25, 1784	January 10, 1846

Names and Dates of People Buried in Old Hurley Burial Grounds

NAME	BIRTH	DEATH
Elting, Solomon	July 9, 1742	July 10, 1809
Catherine, his wife	March 9, 1750	May 31, 1799
Cornelius	November 14, 1745	October 3, 1820
Blandina Elmendorf, his wife	January 5, 1755	November 23, 1820
Hannah	December 10, 1789	January 10, 1837
Solomon C.	July 6, 1787	February 28, 1831
Jane	October 30, 1821	December 11, 1847
Maxon, Horace	September 6, 1818	October 14, 1902
Catherine J. Henion, his wife	December 31, 1822	August 12, 1873
Mary D., their daughter	1851	March 11, 1854
Mary, their daughter	December 1856	March 21, 1857
Elsworth, Abram, Co. C, 156 Regt. NY	July 1816	January 21, 1899
Hester Bush, his wife	1825	February 13, 1887
Frank	1876	1910
William H., Co. A, 120 Regt. NYSV	July 16, 1818	April 30, 1904
Elizabeth W. Wheeler, his wife	1819	January 20, 1900
John E., Co. E, 100 Regiment NYSV	1845	1905
Fankana, Lydia	1833	1907
Ten Eyck, Captain Mattys	March 18, 1658	July 6, 1741
Janntje	Unknown	June 23, 1726
Abraham	October 31, 1689	August 18, 1747
Matthew	February 23, 1728	June 11, 1809
Cornelia Wynkoop, his wife	May 13, 1732	September 2, 1793
Blandina, their daughter	January 17, 1768	January 1, 1837
Maria, their daughter	September 26, 1772	August 9, 1781
Dr. Richard	February 1,1762	February 15, 1851
Janet Baker, his wife	February 4, 1768	November 29, 1823

NAME	BIRTH	DEATH
Pawling, Gitty Ten Eyck,		
wife of Albert Pawling	November 21, 1756	May 23, 1789
Matthew Ten Eyck	May 16, 1787	January 6, 1814
Veder, Abraham, son of		
Matthew and Marie	July 28, 1819	June 29, 1824
Wynkoop, Maj. Adrian	1730	May 16, 1795
Catherine Louw, his wife	January 25, 1733	November 17, 1796
Peter P.	February 1780	October 11, 1847
Herdenburgh	June 30, 1811	August 28, 1844
Wynkoop, Rachel		
Elmendorf, wife of Jacob P.	Unknown	February 14, 1812
Colonel Cornelius D.	March 6, 1734	December 4, 1792
Dirck C.	April 6, 1783	October 5, 1838
Elizabeth Sparling, his wife	January 31, 1777	March 28, 1837
Silinda Crispell, wife of		
Derick C.	February 1821	December 22, 1838
George	March 14, 1814	February 20, 1867
Eleanor S. Davis, his wife	September 12, 1813	January 18, 1846
Ann Hardenburgh, wife		
of Cornelius E.	August 18, 1787	April 15, 1857
Ostrander, Johannis	1723	September 20, 1789
Mary Davis, his wife	Unknown	January 22, 1824
John	April 4, 1774	February 28, 1868
Nelly Roosa, his wife	November 24, 1779	March 4, 1857
Maria	January 4, 1771	November 20, 1856
Samuel	August 25, 1780	May 8, 1854
Dr. Stephen Nottingham	1803	June 2, 1840
Ann, his wife	Unknown	Unknown
Rachel Elmendorf, wife of		
Jacob P.	September 2, 1779	February 14, 1812

Name	Birth	Death
Newkirk, Cornelius Jr.	September 12, 1780	October 20, 1867
Magdalena, his wife	April, 27, 1782	November 3, 1815
Christopher	April 8, 1806	January 10, 1828
Sara	October 5, 1810	March 13, 1841
Sarah Kiersted, wife of Cornelius Newkirk	September 8, 1751	April 29, 1810
Helen M. Lowe, wife of Benjamin Newkirk	November 20, 1806	August 18, 1845
Helen M., their daughter	October 14, 1844	January 1, 1847
Coenradt	April 23, 1723	January 25, 1805
Anne De Witt, his wife	March 4, 1725	October 12, 1805
Andrew	March 14, 1768	March 26, 1826
Lane Lowe, his wife	December 5, 1779	March 30, 1843
Margaret	August 24, 1754	June 28, 1839
Marie Roosa, wife of Garret B.	July 16, 1773	August 8, 1848
Jenette B. daughter of Philip and Phoebe	February 6, 1836	April 4, 1840
Hardenburgh, Jacobus	December 17, 1733	August 11, 1794
Catrina Elting, his wife	Unknown	Unkown

NAME	BIRTH	DEATH
du Bois, Richard	May 8, 1799	May 11, 1869
Catherine Van Vliet, his wife	January 16, 1801	May 7, 1857
John P.	1761	July 21, 1854
Peter	March 29, 1749	April 2, 1830
Arjantje Newkirk, his wife	December 27, 1748	August 25, 1805
Judith, their daughter	March 8, 1784	August 1, 1845
Sarah Mariah, daughter of Richard and Catherine	January 2, 1824	April 1, 1843
Lenah	December 25, 1788	January 21, 1845
Cornelius	January 24, 1743	June 24, 1829
Geertje Van Vliet, his wife	September 4, 1737	May 24, 1819
Maria, their daughter	December 17, 1769	April 27, 1839
Judith, their daughter	January 21, 1776	April 19, 1839
Derick	September 2, 1778	December 24, 1856
Evaline Van Vliet Suyland, his wife	June 9, 1789	October 14, 1868
Harriet A., their daughter	November 13, 1825	February 17, 1827
Harriet A. their daughter,	March 1, 1828	January 17, 1832
Robert W.	November 27, 1817	January 21, 1840
Mary	April 10, 1823	October 12, 1847
Theodore	November 23, 1819	February 9, 1882
Nelly Ann, his wife	May 8, 1827	August 22, 1860
Edmund A.	April 8, 1812	July 10, 1886
John S., son of Derick & Evaline	August 14, 1834	August 26, 1863
John J.	July 31, 1752	April 7, 1832
du Bois, Gitty	September 6, 1802	July 26, 1823
John	June 11,1771	December 1, 1847
John	September 4, 1783	May 24, 1819

Name	Birth	Death
Houghtaling, Thomas	August 2, 1805	October 20, 1897
Eliza G. Hendricks, his wife	September 20, 1803	January 29, 1882
John N.	August 20, 1832	February 1, 1917
Catherine M. Davis, his wife	June 27, 1834	March 25, 1901
Jerome	1849	1907
Mariette Post, his wife	1853	Unknown
Egbert	August 17, 1794	November 2, 1870
Helena Phillips, his wife	March 13, 1792	May 6, 1860
Jeremiah	April 30, 1758	April 14, 1820
Maria Roosa, his wife	January 27, 1766	April 27, 1829
Elizabeth	1797	1797
Boddington, Mary Houghtaling, wife of Edwin	February 11, 1836	February 6, 1870
Thomas, their son	July 24, 1869	November 28, 1869
Brink, Petrus	October 3, 1738	December 31, 1818
Catharina Du Mond, his wife	December 31, 1740	March 10, 1829
Peter	May 12, 1765	July 21, 1841
Rachel Edmoson, his wife	1773	November 24, 1834
Sa Mar	1769	1778
John E.	May 5, 1809	August 12, 1845
Abraham De Witt , his son	October 1838	June 8, 1847
Sarah Jane, his daughter	July 2,1841	November 3,1847
T. Brink	1719	1775
H	1715	May 2, 1779
Van Vliet, Margaret Brown, wife of George	September 1758	March 1833
Meriett, Morris	1776	August 19, 1829
Underhill	1804	December 21, 1830
Mory, Gloriana, wife of Joseph Mory	1764	March 30, 1820

NAME	BIRTH	DEATH
Suyland, Johannis Eunice, his wife	17?? June 11,1766	March 13, 1821 December 1, 1850
Roe, James	June 10, 1790	April 22, 1823
Low, Cornelius, son of Timothy Low	1724	February 17, 1731
Searle, Joshua, son of Jesse and Jerusha	May 30, 1841	October 10, 1841
Sammons, John	1813	September 12, 1845
Lewis, Simeon Phoebe J. Krom, his wife	1819 July 12, 1832	February 14, 1857 Unknown
Murdock, Mary	December 4, 1777	March 27, 1854
Weeks, James Gilbert Charlotte More, his wife William H.	June 20, 1835 September 23, 1835 February 25,1875	September 23, 1900 December 20, 1899 May 5, 1880
Cole, Minner Tunis Janatje Delameter, his wife Cornelius Catherine, his wife William P. Richard Rachel Brink, his wife Jacobus William P. Margaret Oliver, his wife Maria Matthew O. **Cole, Estella**	1809 1727 1733 January 10, 1753 December 1754 November 23, 1778 1784 January 16, 1773 March 8, 1765 November 23, 1778 1828 1811 1860 1858	1900 February 6, 1768 April 6, 1822 October 26, 1817 January 16, 1838 October 17, 1855 August 12, 1845 September 16, 1841 November 8, 1846 October 17, 1855 1911 1881 1867 1918

NAME	BIRTH	DEATH
Teal, William A.	July 21, 1789	November 14, 1854
Catherine A., his wife	April 14, 1792	January 15, 1866
Wygant, Anthony	March 9, 1787	March 17, 1828
Jemima, wife of Lewis Wygant	July 21, 1804	May 19, 1840
Henion, Hiram O.	October 31, 1819	June 22, 1848
Maxson, Abraham	March 17, 1821	June 21, 1850
Daniel	November 7, 1793	May 1, 1828
Jane	September 14, 1800	February 24, 1841
Ezra	October 20, 1823	June 7, 1845
Sarah Ann Davis, his wife	1822	February 6, 1894
Merritt, Rebecca Rose, wife of Caleb Merritt	November 4, 1776	March 31, 1850
Delamater, David	November 20, 1743	September 2, 1795
Dewald, Matilda, daughter of Peter and Elizabeth	March 17, 1859	October 23, 1866
Oliver, Richard Esq.	February 22, 1752	November 1, 1806
Smith, Gardner	1822	October 27, 1891
Jane Cole, his wife	October 12, 1814	January 11, 1874
Elizabeth	1834	1841
William	1836	1841
William	1843	1844
Richard G.	September 20, 1838	September 6, 1874
RDW	Unknown	March 13, 1713

NAME	BIRTH	DEATH
Conway, Matthew, son of Jacob J. and Sarah Conway	September 1844	March 9, 1849
John H., son of Jacob and Sarah	November 1846	March 4, 1849
Vandermark, James, Co. K, 20 Regt. NYC	1835	December 29, 1901
Warner, Charles, son of William and Rachel	May 6, 1842	January 23, 1844
Acker, Andrew, Co. C, 20 Regt. NYC	1821	February 6, 1875
Pattison, Catherine, wife of Abel Pattison	1778	April 1, 1851
Hannah, wife of Abel	March 28, 1818	June 30, 1850
Lorenzo	April 19, 1826	February 13, 1827
Hoffman, Melamcthon, son of Luthor and Ann	November 4, 1844	February 12, 1845
Hendricks, John L.	November 170	October 7, 1841
Elizabeth, his wife	June 21, 1779	November 21, 1854

NOTES

Introduction

1. *Holland Society Yearbook.*

Chapter One

2. Fried, *Early History*.
3. Ibid.
4. Ibid.
5. Ibid.
6. Ibid.
7. Ibid.
8. Ibid.
9. Ibid.
10. Ibid.
11. Information courtesy of the Hudson River Valley Institute.
12. Cregier, *Journal.*
13. Fried, *Early History*, 64.
14. Ibid.
15. Ibid.
16. Ibid.
17. Hofler, *Lost Village*.

18. Fried, *Early History.*
19. Ibid.
20. *Olde Ulster,* "New Paltz Patent."
21. Christophe, *Dungan Papers*, vol. 2, x.
22. Hurley Deedbook, EE, 376.
23. Information courtesy of Hurley Patentee Lighting.
24. De Geer, "1st and 2nd Generations."
25. *Olde Ulster*, "The Divorce of Annetje Arians."
26. Fried, *Early History*.
27. Van Wagenen, "Geneology."
28. Schoonmaker, *History of Kingston.*

CHAPTER TWO

29. Clearwater, *Hurley Days of Slavery.*
30. Schmidt, Letter.
31. Kent, "Schoonmaker."
32. *Olde Ulster*, "Unknown," 22.
33. Ibid.
34. New York (State) Secretary's Office, *Calendar of Land Papers*.
35. *Olde Ulster*.
36. Ibid.
37 Congress, *Biographical Directory*.
38. Benson, *Abraham Van Deusen.*

CHAPTER THREE

39. Breiner, *New York, Ontario.*
40. Nash, "Old Stone Church."
41. Hurley Deed Book BB, 368.
42. Sylvester, *History.*
43. Clearwater, *Hurley Days of Slavery.*

BIBLIOGRAPHY

Benson, Charles B. *Abraham Van Deusen and Many of His Descendants with Biographical Notes 1635–1901.* New York: New York Geneological and Biographical Society, 1980.

Breiner, Charles M. *New York, Ontario and Western Railway.* Middletown, NY: Ontario and Western Railway Historical Society, 1987.

Christophe, Peter L., ed. *New York Historic Manuscripts: Administrative Papers of Governors Richard Nicolls and Frances Lovelace (1664–1678).* Vol. XXII. Baltimore, MD: Genealogical Publishing Co., 1980.

———. *New York Historic Manuscripts: The Dungan Papers.* Vol. I. Baltimore, MD: Geneaological Publishing Co, 1980.

Clearwater, Olive, and John Hofler. *Hurley in the Days of Slavery.* Hurley, NY: Self-published, 1986.

Cregier, Captain Martin. *Journal of the Second Esopus War* (June 1663). www.hudsonrivervalley.org (accessed April 2009).

De Geer, Kent. "The 1st and 2nd Generations of the Ostrander Family." *Ostrander Family Association Newsletter* (2008): 1–12.

Evers, Alf. *The Catskills From Wilderness to Woodstock*. Woodstock, NY: Overlook Press, 1982.

Fried, Marc B. *The Early History of Kingston and Ulster County*. New York: Publishing Center for Cultural Resources, 1975.

Hofler, John. *The Lost Village of HalfWay Ground*. www.hurleyheritagesociety.org/Hurleynews/halfwgnd.htm (accessed January 23, 2006).

Hurley Patentee Lighting. www.hurleypatenteelighting.com (accessed October 26, 2006).

Kent, Don. "Schoonmaker Buys Former Van Sickle Store Property." *Hurley Guardian*, 1947.

Nash, George W. "Old Stone Church at Hurley, NY." *Olde Ulster* (June 1912):171–79.

———. "The Old Stone School House at Hurley." *Olde Ulster* (July 1912): 198.

New York (State) Secretary's Office. *Calendar of NY Colonial Manuscripts Endorsed Land Papers in the Office of the Secretary of the State of New York 1643–1803*. Harrison, NY: Harbor Hill Books, 1987.

Olde Ulster. "Daniel Taylor, the British Spy." January 1905: 238–45.

———. "The Divorce of Annetje Arians." July 1911: 207–12.

———. "Indian Deed to Thomas Chambers." January 1905: 77–83.

———. "The New Paltz Patent." January 1905: 105–14.

Schmidt, James M. Letter, April 22, 1987.

Schoonmaker, M. *The History of Kingston, New York: From Its Early Settlement to the Year 1820*. New York: Burr Printing House, 1888.

Sylvester, Nathaniel Bartlett. *History of Ulster County New York 1662–1880*. Philadelphia: Everts & Peck, 1880.

Ulster County Encyclopedia (1989).

United States Congress. *Biographical Directory of U.S. Representatives.* www.bioguide.congress.gov (accessed April 24, 2009).

Van Wagenen, Carl S. "The Genealogy of Jacob Aertsen Van Wagenen of Wagengen, Holland 1637–1994." Interlaken, NY: Windswept Press, 1994.

Yearbook of the Holland Society. New York: Executive Office, 1902.

ABOUT THE AUTHOR

Deana F. Decker has lived in Hurley for the past thirteen years. Her lifelong interest in history, especially that of Hurley, led to her appointment as town historian in November 2007. Decker is a member of the New York State Association of Public Historians and the Hurley Heritage Society, where she also acts as a docent at their museum. In addition to her history pursuits, she volunteers with the Hurley Fire Department, as well as at the Ernest C. Myer Elementary School. This is her second book on Hurley.

Visit us at
www.historypress.net